The Blue Vein Society

THE BLUE VEIN SOCIETY

SOCIETY

CLASS AND COLOR WITHIN BLACK AMERICA

SAM KELLEY

The Blue Vein Society and *No Hidin' Place* are published by Samuel L. Kelley
P. O. Box 5336 Cortland, NY 13045
samkelley48@hotmail.com
sam.kelley@cortland.edu

Library of Congress Control Number: 2013900383
ISBN: Hardcover   978-1-4797-7576-7
               Softcover   978-1-4797-7575-0
               Ebook   978-1-4797-7577-4

To order additional copies of this book, contact:
Xlibris Corporation
1-888-795-4274
www.Xlibris.com
Orders@Xlibris.com
119186

Additional plays available by Sam Kelley

Pill Hill

White Chocolate

Thruway Diaries

Faith, Hope and Charity: The Story of Mary McLeod Bethune

For Elnora Kelley, whose compassion and generous spirit has made the world a better place.

CONTENTS

FOREWORD...XIII
    JOEL SHATZKY

ACKNOWLEDGMENTS XIX

THE BLUE VEIN SOCIETY 1

THE BLUE VEIN SOCIETY
    BACKGROUND AND PRODUCTION HISTORY...................49

NO HIDIN' PLACE 51

CLASS AND COLOR WITHIN BLACK AMERICA........................86
    SAMUEL L. KELLEY

CHARLES WADDELL CHESNUTT 95

ABOUT THE PLAYWRIGHT 101

Looking down the vista of time I see an epoch in our nation's history, not in my time or yours, but in the not distant future, when there shall be in the United States but one people, moulded by the same culture, swayed by the same patriotic ideals, holding their citizenship in such high esteem that for another to share it is of itself to entitle him to fraternal regard; when men will be esteemed and honored for their character and talents. When hand in hand and heart with heart all the people of this nation will join to preserve to all and to each of them for all future time that ideal of human liberty which the fathers of the republic set out in the Declaration of Independence, which declared that all men are created equal, the ideal for which Garrison and Phillips and Sumner lived and worked; the ideal for which Lincoln died, the ideal embodied in the words of the Book which the slave mother learned by stealth to read, with slow-moving finger and faltering speech, and which I fear that some of us have forgotten to read at all-the Book which declares that "God is no respecter of persons, and that of one blood hath he made all the nations of the earth."

—Charles Waddell Chesnutt
Race Prejudice; Its Causes and Its Cure (1905)

FOREWORD

I first met Sam Kelley in the early eighties, a couple of years after his arrival at the State University of New York (SUNY) College at Cortland. It was following a production of a play titled *Pill Hill,* which Kelley wrote, directed, and played one of the two major leads. I was excited to discover another fellow playwright teaching at Cortland. When I first arrived at the college, there were several faculty colleagues who "wrote plays," some of which were poetic and arresting on the page, but they did not "translate" very well on stage. Even reading *Pill Hill,* one might wonder whether or not it would "translate" on the stage, something true of Eugene O'Neill's work, where the dialogue might appear somewhat awkward and "stagey." However, in watching *Pill Hill* in performance, one notices right away that it comes alive through dialogue. Indeed, Kelley had "heard" with that ear for dialogue that we who write for the stage rather than appearance on the page know so well: the resonance and nuance of the spoken word.

Kelley's family background is a remarkable story in itself, and I believe that it gave him the experience he needed to become a chronicler, not just of the "Black Experience" but of the "human condition"—something all significant drama reveals. Kelley, along with seven of his nine siblings, was adopted and raised by a childless aunt and uncle, Wesley and Gertrude Kelley, on a farm near Marvell, Arkansas, in Phillips County, located in the heart of the Mississippi Delta. Landing in Arkansas shortly before his sixth birthday, Kelley and his older siblings were sent to the fields to chop cotton on the farm, which Uncle Wesley and Aunt Gertrude rented. What was supposed to have been a temporary stay in Arkansas that came about when Kelley's mother was stricken with schizophrenia turned into a double tragedy less than five years later when his father, Booker T. Kelley, died following an operation from a brain tumor. Wesley and Gertrude had wanted a family of their own, but they could not have envisioned the answer to their prayers arriving in the form of a double family tragedy.

Buoyed by their unyielding faith in God and an indefatigable work ethic, Wesley and Gertrude fully embraced the challenge of raising their new family at a time when most couples would be looking forward to retirement and enjoying their grandchildren. The family attended church every Sunday. Wesley Kelley was a church deacon, and Gertrude was very active as a church mother. Kelley vividly recalls his first major performance of James Weldon Johnson's "The Creation" from *God's Trombones* in the eighth grade at St. Luke Missionary Baptist Church, the family place of worship, a couple of miles down the road in Turkey Scratch, Arkansas. Kelley's love of acting had begun in first grade when his teachers put him on the stage, followed by a lead role the next year in the second grade.

Unfortunately, for Kelley, growing up on the farm was not an easy life. He proved to be allergic to the dust in raw cotton, which led to severe asthma. So Kelly was allowed to stay home on some mornings until the dew dried on the cotton. At times, the asthma appeared life-threatening, but there was little relief until Kelley left for college and later moved away permanently.

Wesley and Gertrude's commitment to educating their children matched their faith and work ethic. When the first one went off to college, Wesley Kelley was in his sixty-first year, and when the last finished, he was in this eightieth year. Educated in the segregated school system of Arkansas, Kelley and his siblings demonstrated that an environment in which learning is respected and revered can triumph over many obstacles. Of Kelley's nine siblings, eight earned college degrees, with six having completed graduate and professional degrees—including business, education, medicine, and divinity. Kelley's twin brother is a physician, one of five among the extended family.

After having received a PhD from the University of Michigan, and later becoming tenured at SUNY Cortland, Kelley pursued his playwriting interests at the Yale School of Drama, receiving his MFA in playwriting in 1990. While at Yale, Kelley's play, *Pill Hill*, was selected for a Yale Winterfest production by then Dean Lloyd Richards, a director and mentor to playwright August Wilson. Among other playwrights being produced at the time Kelley was at Yale were Athol Fugard, John Guare, Lee Blessing, Derek Walcott, and others. Fellow playwriting students included Elizabeth Egloff and future Pulitzer Prize winner Lynn Nottage.

Pill Hill, a play about Chicago steel workers who leave the mill to pursue other careers and return to one of their homes occasionally for a reunion, has been produced throughout the country and has received numerous awards including the prestigious Joseph Jefferson Award in the Chicago production in 1994 for Best Ensemble Performance. John Beer, drama critic for Time Out Chicago, wrote of a 2009 production: "*Pill Hill* draws a corrosive picture of individual lives caught within merciless social systems. Racism haunts the men's periodic get-togethers, most pointedly in a monologue about a Southern excursion gone terribly wrong. Writing at the height of the Reagan-Bush years, Kelley saw clearly the impact of right-wing policies on the urban working class." *Pill Hill* was also given a favorable review by Mel Gussow in the *New York Times* in its Hartford Stage production in 1992: "*Pill Hill*, by Samuel Kelley, is a penetrating study of the aspirations and defeats of a group of young working-class black men in Chicago."

Among Kelley's plays that have received readings and productions are *Ain't Got Time to Die* (*August Revival*) (Juneteenth Festival, University of Louisville, 1999); *White Chocolate* (Billie Holiday Theatre, Brooklyn, NY, 2002); *Faith, Hope and Charity: The Story of Mary McLeod Bethune* (Juneteenth Legacy Theatre Bold Journeys Tour (2004); *Thruway Diaries* (Jubilee Theatre, Fort Worth Texas, 2005); and a staged reading of one of his most ambitious plays to date: *Habeas Corpus* (Juneteenth Legacy Theatre 10th Anniversary Jamboree of New Plays, Louisville, Kentucky, 2009) about the Elaine, Arkansas, Race Riot of 1919. The results of the trial ended up in the Supreme Court, with the Court ruling in the black prisoners' favor. Kelley is currently completing a comedy and has begun work on a play about African American women suffragists and voting rights, which is inspired by a true story in Florida.

About the two plays represented in this volume, *Blue Vein Society* was actually Kelley's first produced play by a theater company, receiving its debut performance with the Paul Robeson Performing Arts Company in Syracuse, New York, in 1988. That actually followed a workshop production during Kelley's first semester at the Yale School of Drama. In conversation, he generously credits me with having introduced him to the writings of Charles W. Chesnutt (1858-1932), the early twentieth-century African American short story writer whose tale, "The Wife of His Youth," formed the basis for Kelley's play. The play is a powerful rendering of an experience familiar to many immigrant families when the head of the household leaves the "Old Country" with intentions of sending for the family once he has made his fortune and sometimes becomes "involved" with someone he meets in the "New World." The movie *Hester Street* (1975), directed by Joan Macklin Silver and based on a short story by the novelist and journalist Abram Cahan, is an example of such an experience.

In *Blue Vein Society*, however, the "Old Country" is the antebellum South and the "immigrant" is a former fugitive slave, Josh Ryder—now a "respectable" bourgeois and president of a society in which, among other membership requirements, the candidate must be freeborn and preferably fair enough to be a member of the Blue Vein Society. Ryder is about to marry a light-skinned school teacher, Molly Dixon, who could pass for white. Ryder's snobbery and internalized racism is revealed when his "wife from slavery," Liza Taylor, shows up at his door at just about the time he is planning to announce his engagement to Molly. The ensuing revelations, which include a very moving reminiscence between Josh and Liza of their love for each other, end up leaving Ryder bereft both of his past and future. Liza's presence forces Ryder to come to grips with his identity and painful past, a challenge with which many African Americans struggle as they became members of the growing middle class. Another significant quality in the play that is reflective in both the life of Chesnutt and playwright Kelley is the focus on a strong work ethic, that of African Americans who have worked their way up from their bootstraps to become successful, very typical of all Americans in their pursuit of the American Dream.

As moving and emotionally complex as is *Blue Vein Society*, the newly written companion piece in this volume, *No Hidin' Place*, also based on a short story by Chesnutt, "The Sheriff's Children," is a tense, riveting series of dramatic moments in which an innocent black man is about to be hanged by a lynch mob, his only protection being the local sheriff, who is torn between his personal integrity and the dangers he and his daughter face at the hands of the angry mob. Its examination of the psychology underlying lynching of African Americans and that all too sensitive subject of miscegenation captures the spirit of the heart and mind of early twentieth-century America. I will reveal no further details about the work except to assure the reader that the ending is one of the most powerful and morally complex of any I have read. This debut of the text of *No Hidin' Place* to the reading public offers an excellent opportunity for producers and directors to bring it fully to the stage, possibly as a companion piece to *Blue Vein Society*.

Kelley has also written plays that do not have as their center the African-American experience. One is about the traumas of Parkinson's disease and another on the trauma of retirement. What is most arresting in all of his work, however, is the passion with which Kelley's characters express their dreams, register their disappointments, and their unexpected triumphs.

Joel Shatzky, Professor Emeritus
State University of New York College at Cortland
December 2012

ACKNOWLEDGMENTS

I received my first playwriting assignment for the Yale School of Drama some weeks ahead of the start of school. The assignment required the entering class of playwrights to arrive with a summary or treatment of their first play, which was to be a one act based on a work of fiction that had been published early in the twentieth century, before 1910 as I recall. The time frame was chosen to avoid the problem of copyright infringement.

Excited? Yes! But my excitement was tempered by another reality, finding an African American writer that had achieved national prominence in American literary circles, particularly short fiction. I mentioned my dilemma to fellow colleague Joel Shatzky, a literature professor at the State University of New York (SUNY) College at Cortland, and he suggested Charles Waddell Chesnutt. Luckily, Chesnutt's short story collection, *The Wife of His Youth*, was in my college library. The first story in the collection, also titled "The Wife of His Youth," held my attention from the first paragraph. I didn't stop until I had completed the entire collection. Without a doubt, my first play at Yale would be based on "The Wife of His Youth."

From the very beginning of the first workshop production at Yale, *The Blue Vein Society* was a hit. It continues to be so to this very day. I am particularly indebted to those who have played a role in its success, including theater companies and college programs that have produced the play. Some of these companies and individuals have been noted earlier in reference to my recently published *Thruway Diaries*, so their names are familiar to the reader by now. And if they are familiar, it is because I have developed a relationship with some of the directors, producers, educators, and other theatre professionals over the years. Thanks to them all. I did want to add Barbara Vojta Best, who produced *The Blue Vein Society* at the Strolling Players in Albuquerque and Rio Rancho, New Mexico. She did an amazing job of involving students in the production at Cibola High School in Albuquerque, New Mexico, during the run there. Thanks also to those who have directed productions of *The Blue Vein Society* over the years.

Once again, as with *Thruway Diaries,* I must thank the Paul Robeson Performing Arts Company of Syracuse, New York, especially William Rowland II and Annette Adams-Brown, who served as executive artistic director and associate director respectively at the time of the most recent production. Annette has played major roles in three of my productions at Paul Robeson, including *The Blue Vein Society.* Not only is she a talented actress, but she is talented in the areas of costume and set design, not to mention the related areas of marketing and management required to keep a community theatre running.

A special thanks to Ryan Travis, a very talented actor and playwright, who was completing his MA in African American Studies at Syracuse University at the time of this production. Ryan played the lead in *The Blue Vein Society.* He also played the lead in *Sweat,* which was produced on the bill as the second one act with *The Blue Vein Society.* Subsequent to completing his studies at Syracuse, Ryan went on to complete his MFA in acting at the University of Florida in Gainesville. Thanks to Tina Romaine, stage manager, and also to Kristina Miranovic for her powerful rendition of Molly. Anne Childress, now a graduate student in Africana Studies at Syracuse University, also helped in the proofing and editing in the earlier stages of the preparation for this publication. Yes, I must repeat here something that I mentioned in *Thruway Diaries* in my acknowledgments to Paul Robeson Performing Arts Company: The many years during which I was involved with Paul Robeson Performing Arts Company as a playwright, director, actor, and board member have been your company's gift and your inspiration to me. Once again, I must acknowledge my friend and colleague Joel Shatzky for not only being the one who introduced me to Chesnutt, but also for reading and critiquing the script for both *The Blue Vein Society* and *No Hidin' Place.*

Finally, a very special note of thanks goes to Deborah Williams, retired communication studies secretary at SUNY Cortland, for her generous contribution to that all important task of proofreading. Deborah even typed an earlier version of the manuscript, as I recall. Even after all eyes have read and reread, and proofed again, Deborah manages to find those mistakes overlooked by even the best copyeditors, proofreaders, and writers. Thank you, Deborah.

The Blue Vein Society

Society

CLASS AND COLOR WITHIN
BLACK AMERICA

PAUL ROBESON PERFORMING ARTS COMPANY
BLUE VEIN SOCIETY
20TH ANNIVERSARY PRODUCTION

The Paul Robeson Performing Arts Company produced *The Blue Vein Society* in October 2008 with the following artists and production staff:

CAST

Josh Ryder ....Ryan Travis
Molly Dixon .... Kristina Miranovic
Liza Taylor... Annette Adams-Brown

PRODUCTION CREW

Stage Manager... Tina Romaine
Set Design..Annette Adams-Brown
Costume Design..Annette Adams-Brown
Lighting ....Ben Robinson
Stage Properties..Anne Childress
Set Construction ....Stanley E. Adams
Set Painter... Darnell Williams
Stage Hands .... Anita Sims, Roland Sims
Darnell Williams

COMPANY ARTISTS AND STAFF

William H. Rowland II ....Producer
Executive Artistic Director
Annette Adams-Brown .... Associate Artistic Director
Marcia L. Hagan ....Office Coordinator
Jackie Warren Moore... Teaching Assistant
Resident Poet
Jeffrey Johnson .... Set Construction
Ben Robinson...Light and Sound Technician
Susan Keeter.. Graphic Artists
Cover Design
Fatimah Salaam ....Box Office
Annette Adams-Brown .... Program Layout and Design
Marjorie Wilkins .... Photographer
Anita Sims... Administrative Assistant

THE BLUE VEIN SOCIETY

TIME: 1890

SETTING: Groveland, Ohio.
Rear veranda and yard of Josh Ryder's home.
Afternoon.

CHARACTERS

Josh Ryder: Light brown to fair in complexion; about fifty years old; railroad station master; president of the Groveland Social Society.

Molly Dixon: Very fair in complexion—could pass for white; Twenty-seven; local school teacher; Ryder's fiancé.

Liza Taylor: Dark-skinned, early sixties; Ryder's wife from slavery.

At rise. Molly is seated at table, addressing envelopes. She hums a happy tune. Ryder enters, caressing a bouquet of freshly picked red roses. He waltzes quietly up to Molly from behind, playfully caressing roses as if holding a dancing partner. When he is right behind her, he conceals his bouquet with one hand and taps Molly lightly on the shoulder with the other. She shrieks in fright, then reprimands.

MOLLY: Ah! Josh Ryder, don't do that! You frightened me out of my wits.

Ryder passes bouquet to Molly.

RYDER: I'll bet these *frighten* you too, love.
MOLLY: Um . . . These are my favorite.

Ryder takes Molly by the hand.

RYDER: They don't compare with my favorite rose.
MOLLY: Fresh from your garden.
RYDER: My rose is charming! Beautiful!

(*Taking Molly's hand*)

Stand up.

Molly makes a feeble attempt to resist.

MOLLY:	Josh . . .
RYDER:	Come, my love.
MOLLY:	I have to finish the invitations.
RYDER:	They can wait.
MOLLY:	We've got to get them in the mail today.

Ryder wins out against Molly's resistance as she succumbs to his charm.

RYDER:	Only after I gaze into your lovely eyes.
MOLLY:	I have just two more to go, sweetheart.

Ryder is highly theatrical.

RYDER: My lovely guest of honor! On the night of the society ball, Josh Ryder's home is going to be the most talked about place in Groveland. Servants elegantly attired at the door directing our guests.

(*Thinking out loud*)

I'm going to station the string band in the right parlor—on a raised platform—behind a row of palms. I'll have them play a Strauss waltz as the guests arrive.

(*Taking Molly by the hand and waltzing*)

Molly Dixon and Josh Ryder will take to the floor and get the dancing under way with a lovely waltz. After our beautiful waltz, we'll dine on a supper fit for a queen! After supper, coffee, during which time we'll present the certificates of merit to those who have contributed most to the society's first ever charity ball. It is an expression of our commitment to our less-fortunate brothers and sisters.

(Enjoying a moment of self-deprecating humor)

Forgive me if I appear a bit too modest, but I withdrew from consideration. I've never been one to flaunt my own accomplishments!

Molly responds playfully.

MOLLY: My, dear, you are modest!

Ryder ends dance with flourish.

RYDER: Ah yes, dear! In anticipation of the main event! We'll strike up the band with a resounding drum roll to announce the grand finale!

(Ryder speaks to imaginary ballroom audience, banging spoon against glass, as if speaking to a large crowd.)

"May I have your attention? Thank you. Ladies and gentlemen! The final toast of the evening!"

(To Molly)

Think I'll have Stillman Clearwater introduce me for this one.

(As if Clearwater has introduced him)

"Thank you for that magnificent introduction, Brother Clearwater! Wish to God I knew the whereabouts of the magnanimous gentleman you so aptly described. But I'll be more than happy to stand in for—who did you say? Josh Ryder?

(Proudly)

"Ladies and gentlemen, there is not one among us here tonight of the sterner sex who has not at some time or another in our lives been dependent upon the gentler sex—in infancy for protection, in manhood for companionship, in old age for care and comfort.

(*Molly applauds, lightly amused, genuinely touched by Ryder's speech.*)

"Upon meeting Miss Molly Dixon, Josh Ryder realized he, too, is largely dependent upon woman for most of what makes life worth living—a home, family, friends, and this society. Indeed, this Washington, DC, socialite will grace the society with new standards of culture and taste to which all of us hope to aspire.

Molly can't help but blush with embarrassment at the lavish attention.

MOLLY: Josh . . .

Ryder raises his hands to stop Molly.

RYDER: "Goodness! Dear me . . . I'm getting ahead of myself. Yes! Rumor has it—and it will not be found false. I have the honor this moment of asking for the hand of Miss Molly Dixon! Of presenting to you . . .

(*Holding up ornate box containing ring*)

. . . the engagement ring!"

A breathless Molly stares in surprise and amazement.

MOLLY: You've bought it!

Ryder takes Molly's hand and raises it in the air.

RYDER:	"Ladies and gentlemen!
MOLLY:	Josh!
RYDER:	"I present to you the future Mrs. Josh Ryder!"
MOLLY:	You're wonderful!

Ryder pulls out box, which contains the ring.

RYDER: Here now is the ring that will grace these delicate fingers. A railroad station manager doesn't squander a three-month salary on diamonds.

(*Kissing Molly on the hand*)

No hand ever deserved diamonds more.

MOLLY:	Josh . . .
RYDER:	No, Molly.

Molly can't resist going after the box.

MOLLY:	Let me . . . I want to see my ring!
RYDER:	You'll see it at the ball.
MOLLY:	The ball!
RYDER:	The ball, Molly.
MOLLY:	That's six weeks!
RYDER:	Ah, yes—six weeks.
MOLLY:	That's eternity!

Ryder evades Molly as he moves about, filled with excitement about his plans for the ball.

RYDER: This place will be bursting at the seams!

Molly follows Ryder in hopes of seeing the ring.

MOLLY:	Let me try it on.
RYDER:	People from every respectable calling!

Molly imagines the ring on her finger.

MOLLY: I want it to be a perfect fit.
RYDER: Doctors, lawyers, military officers, teachers.

Molly goes after Ryder again, but he stays out of reach.

MOLLY: Place it on my finger, Josh.
RYDER: They will be here!
MOLLY: Please . . .
RYDER: Yes, at Josh Ryder's, to witness this magnificent occasion!
MOLLY: I want to feel it just once, Josh, before the ball.
RYDER: Bad luck to see the ring before the appointed time.

Molly extends her finger in hopes Ryder will place the ring on it.

MOLLY: I'll close my eyes.
RYDER: Promise?
MOLLY: Promise!
RYDER: Are you sure?

Molly closes her eyes and turns her head away so as to not look at the ring.

MOLLY: Yes, yes! I promise.

Ryder removes ring from box.

RYDER: Eyes closed?
MOLLY: Yes!

Ryder takes Molly's hand and kisses her on the ring finger. She gives off an ecstatic shriek at the touch of his lips, placing her handkerchief against her lips in delight, still turned away.

RYDER: Head over your shoulders! No peeking.
MOLLY: I shan't peek.

Ryder slips ring onto Molly's finger.

RYDER:	There!
MOLLY:	It's a perfect fit!
RYDER:	Perfect, Molly!
MOLLY:	Please! One peek!
RYDER:	No!
MOLLY:	Josh!
RYDER:	We must not spoil the fun before the ball.

Ryder removes ring and places it back into box.

MOLLY:	Don't take my ring, Josh!
RYDER:	There! Will the bride open her eyes? So when do I get to see my favorite rose in her ball gown?

A cheerful Molly responds with wicked delight.

MOLLY:	Not before I see my ring!
RYDER:	Then on with the invitations! Let me have the story for the ball. Did you get it ready for the weekend edition of the *Groveland Press?*
MOLLY:	Yes, dear. You can drop it off when you take the invitations to the post office.

Ryder follows Molly to the table.

RYDER:	Guess who will be the envy of Groveland? Sweetheart, I'm indebted to you for taking care of the finer details of social etiquette for this momentous undertaking.
MOLLY:	I'm honored to do so.

Ryder checks out guests on social registers.

RYDER:	I wouldn't dare trust matters of such taste and sophistication to anyone else but you, dear.
MOLLY:	Well, thank you.

Ryder is suddenly taken aback by the appearance of a name on the list.

RYDER: Molly!

An ill-at-ease Molly tries to sound reassuring.

MOLLY: Oh, Josh—I took the liberty of adding several oversights to the list.

RYDER: Oversights?

MOLLY: I know you didn't mean to overlook Nate and Naomi.

RYDER: Nate is a North Carolina transplant.

MOLLY: Most of us are "transplants," as you say, dear.

RYDER: A transplant with a dubious background.

MOLLY: Dubious background? Nate and Naomi have been here twenty-five years. Naomi heads the First Baptist Missionary Society.

RYDER: Sweetheart, you know I'm up for society president again this year.

MOLLY: The ball wouldn't be the same without Naomi. She's the first person I came to know when I moved to Groveland.

RYDER: I can't afford to upset Mordicai Jones and Stillman Clearwater. See that Nate and Naomi get an invitation to the wedding, but the ball is another matter.

MOLLY: I hardly know a single person on the invitation list.

RYDER: The society has to restrict itself to individuals who have achieved a respectable calling in life. Molly! Charlie Reid!

MOLLY: Charlie Reid is every bit a gentleman.

RYDER: Charlie isn't a society member!

MOLLY: He's the only person in Groveland with a college degree in music.

RYDER: One doesn't need a college degree in music to be a musician!

MOLLY: Josh!

RYDER: Not Charlie Reid, Molly.

MOLLY:	Why not?
RYDER:	You see, our friends—such as Mordicai Jones and Stillman Clearwater—wouldn't appreciate seeing Charlie show up at the ball.
MOLLY:	And why do they object to Charlie's attendance?
RYDER:	Molly, you must understand. The image of the society is extremely important, and Charlie represents a direction in which the society is not yet prepared to move.

Molly's impatience is increasingly transparent.

MOLLY:	Charlie Reid is a decent and honest, God-fearing man.
RYDER:	Don't remind me, please.
MOLLY:	Then why must you object to his attendance?

Ryder is increasingly agitated.

RYDER:	We can't afford to be at odds with the taste and standards of the larger community.
MOLLY:	I take that to mean the whites?
RYDER:	Charlie isn't right for the society—Stillman and Mordicai wouldn't approve.

An exasperated Molly loses her patience.

MOLLY:	Josh Ryder, will you speak directly to the point!

Ryder erupts, shocking Molly.

RYDER:	For heaven's sake, Molly! Charlie Reid is as black as ant guts!
MOLLY:	Josh!
RYDER:	Say yes to Charlie and every black ass nigger in Groveland will be breaking down the doors to join the society!

MOLLY:	Reverend Dexter of the AME Zion Church is more on the African side than Charlie Reid, and he is on this list.
RYDER:	Clearwater and Jones are elders at Reverend Dexter's church.
MOLLY:	And you, Josh? Surely you're not opposed to Charlie's presence?
RYDER:	God forbid! I'd love to have Charlie attend.
MOLLY:	I knew you would! I'll see to it that his invitation goes in the mail with the other invited guests this afternoon.
RYDER:	Wait, Molly.
MOLLY:	Yes?
RYDER:	There is another matter with which I can't quibble.
MOLLY:	Nothing of consequence, I hope.
RYDER:	The society no longer accepts people who cannot show evidence of free birth.

Molly is severely stricken, but Ryder is much too preoccupied to notice.

MOLLY:	Josh!
RYDER:	I didn't make the rules, Molly!
MOLLY:	You never told me free birth is a prerequisite for membership in the society.
RYDER:	It is a rule that was instituted several months after your arrival.
MOLLY:	How regrettable, Josh.
RYDER:	Regrettable, Molly?
MOLLY:	I've spent three months preparing for a ball that shuns the very people the society claims to help.
RYDER:	I didn't write the rules.
MOLLY:	But you're sworn to uphold them.
RYDER:	The society has the right to make known by its exclusiveness the people it wants to attract.
MOLLY:	You're the first person of my race to humiliate me in such a demeaning manner.
RYDER:	Molly, the next time Charlie applies for membership I'll take it upon myself to make sure he is given due

consideration and meets the free birth regulation. Anything short of that and you're asking me to break the rules.

MOLLY: It's not Charlie I'm speaking of.

RYDER: What!

MOLLY: Josh!

Ryder frantically searches through invitations.

RYDER: Good Lord, Molly! Who else is on this list?

MOLLY: Must I hang my head in shame?

A stunned and embarrassed Ryder stares uncomfortably at Molly.

RYDER: Molly, you never told me.

MOLLY: You never asked!

RYDER: I never suspected you. You, of all people, sweetheart! You should have told me.

MOLLY: Told you? Why should I have told you, Josh? For the great privilege of being demeaned and humiliated!

RYDER: No, no, Molly. If I'd known about you, I'd have fought Mordicai and Stillman when they introduced the free birth rule.

MOLLY: Am I the only reason?

RYDER: How was I to know? You were so . . . so . . .

MOLLY: So what, Josh?

RYDER: Beautiful, Molly. That's it! You were so beautiful!

MOLLY: I don't feel obliged to continue addressing invitations to an event to which I am unable to attend because unwritten rules exclude people of my ungodly birth.

RYDER: I'm sorry.

MOLLY: I'm not!

RYDER: Molly—if you have to know the truth . . .

MOLLY: Perhaps I should go.

RYDER: No, you can't!

MOLLY: Tell my one reason why I shouldn't go.

RYDER: You're the reason I said yes to the free birth rule. My only reason! Call me insanely jealous, a

	possessive fool, any ungodly name you want, but I don't want anyone or anything to come between us—not Charlie, Stillman and Mordicai, the society—nothing, Molly!
MOLLY:	Right now, I feel as though I'm standing in the way of your dreams.
RYDER:	Don't say that!
MOLLY:	I'm beneath the standards of taste you've set for the lady in your life.
RYDER:	Molly, since the moment I saw you at the church anniversary, I've wanted to walk down the aisle with you!
MOLLY:	Oh! Josh Ryder! I'll bet you've offered that pathetic line to every eligible lady in Groveland.
RYDER:	Look, Molly!

(*Pointing to rose garden*)

There, roses and more roses! A red rose was growing out of your hair as you stood on the church steps that Sunday morning. You were beaming so radiantly. Tell me you remember it as I do.

(*Molly does not speak, but Josh has clearly touched her heart strings.*)

Roses were all I saw the moment I laid eyes on you. I uprooted the old garden and planted roses for you. I know how silly and romantic it sounds, but it's true. I've never planted roses for anyone but Molly Dixon.

Molly evades Ryder as she struggles with her pain.

MOLLY:	I'll be the loneliest person at the ball.
RYDER:	Oh you mustn't, sweetheart. Nate and Naomi will be there. And so will Charlie. Anybody you choose to invite will be there.

MOLLY:	And what will Mordicai and Stillman say when you violate the society rules? Josh, they might object.
RYDER:	Sweetheart, you've forgotten. It's a charity ball. I'm the society president, and this is one president who's bending the rules to fit the occasion if that's what it takes to rise to the standards of the lady of his dreams. Mordicai and Stillman can stick their heads in the outhouse for all I care.

(Taking Molly by the hand)

So there! It's settled! Now, my precious flower, does Josh Ryder look like a monster anymore? You know what I want for us, Molly? I want us to chase little Josh Ryders through the rose beds. But if they ever pull up a single one of my lady's roses, I'll tan their hides.

Molly offers a token gesture of ineffective resistance.

MOLLY: Perhaps I should freshen up the lemonade.

Ryder pulls Molly close.

RYDER:	Lemonade won't cool the flames that burn within me at this moment.
MOLLY:	I don't know—now that you know about me . . .

Ryder recites "Sonnet CXVI" from Shakespeare with a delightful, unabashed passion that is Ryder at his best.

RYDER: "Let me not to the marriage of true minds
                          Admit impediments . . ."

Molly blushes in embarrassment as she promenades. Ryder steps in sync, following her at a distance.

MOLLY:	Josh . . .
RYDER:	"Love is not love

Which alters when in alteration finds,
Or bends with the remover to remove.
O, no! It is an ever-fixed mark
That looks on tempests and is never shaken.
It is the star to every wandering bark,
Whose worth's unknown, although his height be
taken.
Love's not Time's fool, though rosy lips and cheeks
Within his bending sickle's compass come;
Love alters not with his brief hours and weeks,
But bears it out even to the edge of doom."

An awkward, if embarrassed, Molly can't resist the charming Ryder as he pours it on.

MOLLY: Josh!
RYDER: "If this be error and upon me prove, I never writ, nor no man ever loved."

At the end of the recitation, Ryder has moved to Molly, his eyes caressing hers.

MOLLY: And you're sure you haven't been spilling that line to every eligible lady in Groveland?
RYDER: I save my poetry for my princess.

Molly teases, but there is a wicked reality in her lines that reverberate with the power of a two-edged sword.

MOLLLY: Then look me in the eye. Now, tell me that it's my blue-black skin that you're madly in love with.
RYDER: My dear . . .
MOLLY: My thick lips . . .
RYDER: Miss Dixon . . .
MOLLY: My kinky hair . . .
RYDER: You are . . .
MOLLY: My wide hips . . .

Ryder blushes with delightful embarrassment.

RYDER: The cruelest woman in the world!

They embrace and kiss. While locked in their embrace, a very dark-skinned woman enters. She is in her early sixties, her face scarred with the hardship of many rough years. A relic from the plantation days of slavery, her clothing is noticeably worn but sufficient, even suggesting a certain pride about her. Though tired from the long trip, underneath is a stoicism from which she derives the energy to propel her forward, as she has done for so many years. She carries two traveling bags, both of which have seen many years on the road.

Upon seeing Ryder, the woman clutches her bags uneasily, in fearful anticipation, torn between making a hasty retreat and coming closer to get a better look at his face. As she turns to come closer, her eyes meet Ryder's, over Molly's shoulder. Neither is able to break the searching gaze. Molly senses another's presence and turns to face the woman, clinging affectionately to Ryder's arm. Liza calls out to Ryder in a cautious, breathless surprise, suggesting some possible recognition.

LIZA: Sam?
MOLLY: Excuse me, ma'am, were you looking for someone?
LIZA: Sam . . .

Ryder responds formally, but ever the gentleman.

RYDER: I beg your pardon, ma'am?
LIZA: I's lookin' fer Sam Taylor, my husband.
MOLLY: Oh, this is Josh Ryder's residence.
RYDER: That's right, ma'am, Josh Ryder.
LIZA: Mr. Ryder?
MOLLY: Who did you say you were looking for, ma'am?
LIZA: Sam Taylor, my husband.
MOLLY: You're a bit mixed up in your address, ma'am.
RYDER: I'm Josh Ryder, ma'am.
LIZA: Josh Ryder?
MOLLY: Yes, Josh Ryder.
LIZA: Then you de man I's suppose ta see.
MOLLY: I believe you said Sam Taylor.
LIZA: Yes, ma'am, I did.
RYDER: She looks a bit confused.
MOLLY: And tired, sweetheart.

LIZA: De man at de train station told me ta come to Josh Ryder if I's lookin' fer Sam Taylor 'cause you been heah long's anybody he knows 'bout. Dat's why I came to you, Mr. Ryda, lookin' fer my husband.

Ryder is relieved, if uneasy.

RYDER: Oh, I see. They don't ask questions anymore—just send them straight to Josh Ryder!

LIZA: Yessir, dat's why I came to you, Mr. Ryda, lookin' fer my husband.

Ryder glances around at Molly.

RYDER: Well—

                        (*Clutching Molly around the waist with reassuring affection*)

                        I'm glad we've cleared up that bit of confusion!

LIZA: I is too, Mr. Ryda.

Ryder offers Liza a seat.

RYDER: Welcome to Groveland, Mrs. Taylor.

LIZA: Thank ya, sir.

Liza passes Molly a glass of lemonade.

MOLLY: Sit and rest a spell.

LIZA: I's much obliged to ya, Miss Ryda.

RYDER: Miss Dixon—Molly Dixon . . .

MOLLY: For a short while longer . . .

LIZA: I's wonderin' if you folk heard tell of a man named Sam Taylor goin' 'round to da colored churches askin' 'bout his wife Liza Jane.

RYDER: Don't believe I have, Mrs. Taylor. It *is* Mrs. Taylor?

LIZA: Most evahbody jes calls me Liza.

MOLLY: Where are you coming from, Liza?

LIZA:	I's been on de road some twenty-five years looking fer Sam.
MOLLY:	Twenty-five years, Josh!
RYDER:	Yes—I heard—sweetheart.
LIZA:	Massa went off to de wa and de field hands commenced ta leavin', so I set out fer Sam. You evah heard 'bout Massa Womack, Mr. Ryda?
RYDER:	Don't recollect hearing talk of a Womack plantation in Groveland, Mrs. Taylor.
LIZA:	Den you wouldn't know 'bout Massa Womack's plantation 'cauz it's outside Raleigh.
MOLLY:	Outside Raleigh?
LIZA:	Raleigh, Nawth Calina.
MOLLY:	Oh, I see, North Carolina.
RYDER:	How did you and your husband get separated, Mrs. Taylor?
LIZA:	Massa Womack needed some money, so he figured he's sell Sam to a Alabama speculator for fifteen dollars. Now, dat ain't what 'twas promised in de first place. Massa Womack promised Sam he wuz gwine ta be a free man when he got to be twenty-one, but he went back on his wud when de crops went bad dat yeah. Soon's I got wud of Massa Womack's plans ta sell Sam, I told him, and he made his git away under de cuva of darkness. Dey got togetha a posse and a pack of bloodhounds. Dey wuz out searchin' fer Sam neahbout de whole week.
MOLLY:	Liza, you don't suppose Sam got caught?
LIZA:	Oh no, ma'am! Sam outwitted dat posse—dem bloodhounds too. You see, Old Massa Womack got so mad that he sold me to a Massa Frazier. Said if he couldn't sell Sam, by God he's gonna make sure he got something fer me. My back's lined wid de whelps from de beatin' Massa put on me when he lost Sam, but I's still happy as a lark Sam got his freedom.

(*With unyielding conviction*)

I'd do it again—right now—if dat's what it takes ta keep um from hangin' my Sam.

Molly turns to Ryder.

MOLLY:	It's a shame Sam never went back for Liza.
RYDER:	Let's not speak for Sam, sweetheart.
MOLLY:	You think maybe he went back?
LIZA:	Sam went back, Miss Molly.
MOLLY:	You think so?
LIZA:	Yes, ma'am.
RYDER:	He probably went back after the war, sweetheart.
LIZA:	Sam said he wuz gwine ta come back ta git me—and if Sam said he's comin' back ta git me, he came back. Said he's gwine ta sneak me out if Massa Womack wouldn't let him purchase my freedom. Dat wuzn't ta be as planned. De Wa came between us, and peoples got scattered all ovah de country. I's been all ovah de South—all de way down de cost ta Chalstun, ovah ta de red hill ova Adlanta, amongst de Creoles in New Oiluns, west up through de Tennuhsee mountains, ovah to Chatnooga, and on ta Knoxville and Louisville. I's been thru jes 'bout evah wide place in de road down South. I's all de family Sam's got left. His parents died when he was neahbout five years old. Luella, Massa Womack's cook, took Sam fer her own child and raised him. I suppose you wouldn't know 'bout Miss Luella. Would you, Mr. Ryda?
MOLLY:	Oh no, no, Josh wouldn't know Miss Luella, Liza.
LIZA:	Miss Luella—God rest her soul—she came down wid a deathly case of malaria fever and died. De child died calling out fer Sam.
MOLLY:	Sorry to hear about Miss Luella, Liza . . .
RYDER:	Yes, yes, Mrs. Taylor. Sorry to hear about Miss Luella.
MOLLY:	God rest her soul.
RYDER:	How have you supported yourself all these years, Mrs. Taylor?

Liza takes pride in her occupation.

LIZA:	I's a fine cook. Done cook my way all ovah de South. I's hopin' ta find a nice colored family in Groveland ta take me in till I's able to git wuk in somebody's kitchen.
MOLLY:	You don't have a place to stay, Liza?
LIZA:	No, ma'am, I don't.
MOLLY:	Josh?
RYDER:	I'm sure Mrs. Taylor is returning home as soon as she completes her search for her husband.
LIZA:	Home is where evah I be's when I gits there, Mr. Ryda.
RYDER:	Surely you have other possessions, Mrs. Taylor?
LIZA:	Evah thing I own is right heah in my two travelin' bags. De rest is on my back. I'll be all right soon's I find a place ta stay.
MOLLY:	She needs a place to stay, sweetheart.
RYDER:	If you're going to be in town for a couple of days, there's a modest hotel down by the train station.
MOLLY:	Oh no, no, Josh . . .
RYDER:	I'll be happy to take care of the accommodations for Mrs. Taylor . . .
MOLLY:	I wouldn't let you put yourself to that trouble, sweetheart.
RYDER:	It's no trouble at all, dear.
MOLLY:	I have more than enough room for Liza.
RYDER:	Perhaps you should ask. Mrs. Taylor may want to make it to Groveland before late evening.
MOLLY:	She needs a place to stay for the night. I'll put Liza up with me.
LIZA:	If it ain't too much trouble, Miss Molly, I'd as soon as spend the night restin' my achin' feet.
MOLLY:	It's no trouble at all, Liza.
RYDER:	Oh well, if Mrs. Taylor wishes to stay, I'll be more than happy to put her up here for the night.
MOLLY:	Don't bother, dear.
RYDER:	It's no bother. I'm accustomed to entertaining guests . . .

MOLLY:	It's taken care of. Liza, you're my guest tonight.
LIZA:	I's much obliged to ya, Miss Molly.
MOLLY:	I'm honored! I'll rush over right now and get Jasper to help prepare Liza's room before he leaves for town. It'll only take a few minutes . . .
RYDER:	I'll give you a hand, dear . . .
MOLLY:	Absolutely not! You're to stay here and keep Liza company.
RYDER:	Are you sure you can manage, sweetheart?
MOLLY:	You're the one Liza is here to see. You two get acquainted. I insist!

A gesture of affection is exchanged between Molly and Ryder as Molly excuses herself and departs. Ryder follows her to exit, looking after her for an uncomfortably long moment. He turns to Liza, uneasily.

RYDER:	I hope spending the night with Molly isn't too much trouble for you, Mrs. Taylor.
LIZA:	You reckon I ought ta go and look fer a place somewhere else?
RYDER:	Oh no, Molly and I are delighted to have the pleasure of your company.
LIZA:	I don't wanna be a noose 'round nobody's neck.
RYDER:	No trouble at all. Would you like more lemonade, Mrs. Taylor?
LIZA:	Believe I do. Dat last glass didn't quite hit de spot.

Ryder pours Molly another glass of lemonade.

RYDER:	This climate makes one thirsty.
LIZA:	Ain't it de truf.

Ryder adds a mint leaf to the lemonade, with a gentlemanly flair that shows a touch of admiration.

RYDER:	A touch of mint brings out the flavor.
LIZA:	This Miss Molly's lemonade?
RYDER:	Yes, yes. It sure is.

*Liza sips lemonade, almost as if searching for some revelation through its taste.
She speaks with deliberation.*

LIZA:	It's good and tasty.
RYDER:	Molly makes the finest lemonade.

Liza gazes at house, a mixture of wishful thinking and cautious excitement.

LIZA:	Dis 'bout the finest colored house I's evah been ta.
RYDER:	Thank ya, ma'am. I built it myself, with a little help from boarders I used to take in when I lived in my house on Pilgrim Street. They were mostly young men from down south looking for a temporary place to stay.
LIZA:	Mighty lot of room fer a single man.
RYDER:	I always wanted a fine home, wife, and children.
LIZA:	You's a lot like me 'bout dat. How many rooms you got?

Liza takes in the environs as a pleased Ryder describes his home.

RYDER:	Four bedrooms upstairs. Downstairs there's a piazza that leads to the main entrance hallway. There is a parlor, a dining room in the right rear, a kitchen, a pantry stocked full of food, a bath hall, and a toilet. Yes. And there is a library filled with books.
LIZA:	Running water and a liberry—you must be a professuh?

Ryder can't help but blush with pride in his accomplishments.

RYDER:	No, ma'am. I'm a railroad station manager at Ohio Central. I have been their twenty-five years now—give or take a couple years.
LIZA:	Dat's a long time.
RYDER:	Never missed a day's work in my life.
LIZA:	Dat means you got a strong constitution.

RYDER: Takes a strong back to lift suitcases all day. One day, I was loading this judge's suitcases and he looked at me and said, "Boy, can you read and write?" I wouldn't dare tell him I'd never set foot inside a schoolhouse. "Read and write? Yes, sir! I certainly can!" Next day when I showed up, Manager Wilson called me in and told me he was promoting me to clerk. Fifteen years later, I was promoted to assistant manager. When Manager Wilson retired—God rest his soul—he saw to it that I took his place as manager. Highest position ever earned by a colored in this town.

LIZA: I see you done made somethin' out yoself, Mr. Ryda.

RYDER: Thank you, ma'am.

Liza takes in the garden, noticing rose beds as she speaks.

LIZA: You lay out these heah rose beds?

RYDER: Oh yes, yes.

LIZA: They sho 'nuff pretty.

RYDER: Thank you—used to have Rose of Sharon, but they don't grow too well in this climate.

LIZA: Rose of Sharon, did you say?

RYDER: What?

LIZA: You said Rose of Sharon.

RYDER: Oh, yes. I brought over several plants—over from my Pilgrim Street house when I moved here. They never took root. I watered them, fertilized them, tried everything I could to nourish them back to health, but they just wouldn't take root.

LIZA: They wouldn't take root ova here?

RYDER: Almost as though they were out of their element.

LIZA: Poor things.

RYDER: I dug them up and planted roses.

Liza is taking particular notice of roses on table.

LIZA: Miss Molly like roses?

RYDER:	Molly loves roses.
LIZA:	Red roses.
RYDER:	Red roses.

For a quick moment, Liza and Ryder find themselves staring eye to eye then looking away.

LIZA:	If my eyes wuzn't playing tricks on me . . .
	(Spurt of cautious humor)
	I'd swear by Massa Womack's plantation you's my Sam Taylor!
RYDER:	That's quite all right, Mrs. Taylor. You must understand that you've been looking for your husband for so long until the faces of so many Sam Taylors are running together in your mind.
LIZA:	You reckon dat mean de Lawd's tellin' me to put an end ta my search for Sam?
RYDER:	I'd better not speak for the Lord.
LIZA:	Amen!
RYDER:	More lemonade, Mrs. Taylor?
LIZA:	I's fine now—thank ya.
RYDER:	We have more—if you like.
LIZA:	Dat last glass hit de spot.
RYDER:	You know, Mrs. Taylor, it is entirely possible that your husband may have improved his lot in life far beyond what was expected of a slave.

Liza blurts another spurt of loud laughter.

LIZA:	Lawd today! Mr. Ryda, I see you don't know Sam atall.
RYDER:	I don't?
LIZA:	Nooo, Lawd! Sam wuz de laziest man on Massa Womack's plantation!
RYDER:	Lazy, did you say?
LIZA:	Sam wuzn't wukin' fer nobody callin' hisself a massa ovah him. Dat's why he sneaked and taught hisself how ta read and write when he's supposed to be out

wukin'. Sometimes he'd neahbout scare me ta death 'cause Miss Luella kept sneakin' dem books outta Massa's liberry fer Sam. Massa Womack would a hanged dem both if he'd a got wind of what dey wuz doin'.

RYDER: I'd say any man who outwits Old Man Womack and his pack of bloodhounds is an industrious person.

LIZA: Oh yeah, Sam, he outwitted da possee, de bloodhounds too—sho 'nuff did.

RYDER: I trust you do know that your slave marriage was not legal, Mrs. Taylor.

LIZA: Dat ain't got nothin' ta do wid de way me and Sam feel 'bout each othah. Sam'd nevah let anotha woman come between us long as I wuz alive, Mr. Ryda. De minute Sam sees his Liza, he'll be neahbout breakin' his neck gittin' ta me. I can see him now jes runnin' and yellin' out, "Liza! Liza, honey, dat's my Liza!" Den he'll grab me in his big strong arms and be jes a laughin' dat old big hearty laugh of his. He'll look me in de eyes and hold me close. Then he'll commence his recitation . . .

RYDER: Mrs. Taylor! I hate to blunt your hopes, but have you considered that your husband just might be deceased?

LIZA: Sam ain't dead!

RYDER: Oh, you think not?

LIZA: Naw—didn't you see de way you and Miss Molly commenced ta findin' me a place ta stay no soon's I got heah? Now dat's a sign de Lawd tellin' me Sam's still wid de livin'.

Molly enters, taking note of the weather.

MOLLY: This weather is getting hotter by the minute.

LIZA: Dat means a storm is brewin'.

MOLLY: Can't be. There's not a cloud in the sky. A good rain would keep the roses blooming.

LIZA: Yes, ma'am, it would.

Molly pours another glass of lemonade for Liza.

MOLLY: Another glass for you, Liza.
LIZA: Thank ya, ma'am.
MOLLY: I know how hard it's been on you searching for Sam all these years.
RYDER: Let's not forget how hard it's been on poor Sam.

Molly teases Sam with affection.

MOLLY: "Poor Sam," as if you have a right to know.

                     (*To Liza, with resolve*)

                     Liza, you've searched long enough. From this moment on, Josh and I are going to be your hands and your feet.
RYDER: Molly, I don't want you to burden yourself with the task of finding Sam Taylor.
MOLLY: Burden myself?
RYDER: Listen, Molly, finding Mr. Taylor . . .
MOLLY: Finding *Sam*, sweetheart.
RYDER: Finding Sam could turn out to be a heartrending experience for all of us.
MOLLY: Heartwarming, Josh!
RYDER: You're not listening, Molly!
MOLLY: I'm listening very well, thank you. I've already set the wheels of my search in motion.

Ryder takes Molly aside.

RYDER: Molly, you have a woman here devoted to finding—tracking down—a man she knew from another era in history that's passed and forgotten for most of us.
MOLLY: You're not suggesting Sam would disown his wife.
RYDER: Absolutely not.
MOLLY: You'd better not be, Josh Ryder.

(Playfully scolding Ryder)

	Should something happen to separate us, how long would you wait for me? Five years?
RYDER:	Now, now sweetheart . . .
MOLLY:	Maybe ten?
RYDER:	You're not suggesting . . .
MOLLY:	Fifteen at most?
RYDER:	You're not suggesting men are less loyal than women!
MOLLY:	You most certainly wouldn't wait twenty-five years!
LIZA:	Sam still waiting fer me, Miss Molly.
MOLLY:	How long were you and Sam married before you became separated, Liza?
LIZA:	Two yeahs, fo munths, ten deys, Miss Molly . . .
MOLLY:	Two years, four months, ten days! It could be the most exciting story Groveland has heard since the war. Think about it, dear—the story of a woman who finds her husband from slavery after searching for twenty-five years! How thrilling it must be for them. Sweetheart, we'll introduce Liza and Sam at the society ball as the special guest of honor!
RYDER:	Molly, dear . . .
MOLLY:	I know you're announcing our engagement, but it would be an even greater honor for me to present Sam and Liza at the ball.
RYDER:	Sweetheart . . .
MOLLY:	Think of what it means to this town and to the society? Uniting a couple separated for twenty-five years is the best way in the world to show Mordicai and Stillman that the Groveland Social Society is committed to the social elevation of all our people.
RYDER:	What makes you think Sam will come forward and identify himself?
MOLLY:	He'll come forward—as soon as he hears about his wife. What husband wouldn't?
RYDER:	And if he's not in Groveland, Molly?

MOLLY:	Sweetheart, relax. We've got six weeks before the ball. Here is my plan. We'll contact every prominent colored church in the Midwest—Chicago, Detroit, Cleveland, even St. Louis. I'll get notices out to all the colored newspapers.
RYDER:	Molly, dear . . .
MOLLY:	We'd better include New York and Philadelphia, in case Sam settled in the Northeast. Who knows, maybe California to the west. Just think about it. Sam may have struck a gold mine!
RYDER:	Sweetheart, we can't allow ourselves to be seduced by the romance of what has been a difficult experience for Mrs. Taylor—and for what is bound to be a traumatic experience for Sam. Believe me, Sam and Liza will want to spend their first few weeks at home out of the social spotlight.
MOLLY:	Well! There's certainly no reason why we can't start with the churches right here in Groveland. I'll get the notice out in time for Sunday service. Goodness! Why on earth did I not I remember to ask Nate and Naomi? They've been here longer than anyone I know.
RYDER:	Dear, I believe I saw Nate and Naomi pass by on their way to town this morning.
MOLLY:	They've returned.
RYDER:	Really? How can you be certain?
MOLLY:	I waved to them from the backyard on the way over.
RYDER:	Just now, dear?
MOLLY:	Just now. Will you make the announcement at the society meeting tomorrow?
RYDER:	I'll be happy to.
MOLLY:	Wonderful!
LIZA:	Sam will be heah befo sundown if he gits wud I's in town 'cause we got a heap of catchin' up ta do.
MOLLY:	Liza, Josh and I want you to tell us everything you know about Sam that will aid us in our search.
LIZA:	Sam be 'bout fifty or mo yeahs old now, Miss Molly.

MOLLY:	Close to your age, sweetheart.
RYDER:	Give or take a few good years.
LIZA:	I's a good bit older then Sam, but dat didn't matter 'cauz de minute I laid eyes on him, I knowd I's in love wid um. I tell ya, Miss Molly, de Lawd made my marriage to Sam in de heavun abuv.

A touched Molly turns to Ryder with affection.

MOLLY:	Josh, dear. Sam sounds like a wonderful man!
RYDER:	Yes—a wonderful man.
LIZA:	He sho 'nuff wuz, Miss Molly.
MOLLY:	Liza, you must tell us more about this wonderful man.
RYDER:	It's been a long time, sweetheart . . .
LIZA:	Seems like 'twas jes yestudey when Sam wuz sneaking up behind me, ticklin' me in de sides. Befo' I'd git turned around ta see him, he'd be done grabbed me in his arms, lifting me ovah his head. I'd be way up in de air jes a shouting' and screamin' fer him ta put me down.

(Struggling, near tears)

	Seems like 'twas yesterday, Miss Molly. Don't know how much furtha I can go on looking fer Sam.
MOLLY:	Josh—
	(Overlapping)
RYDER:	Molly—
MOLLY:	Yes, dear?
	(Overlapping)
RYDER:	Yes, dear?
MOLLY:	I was wondering—I'm going over and see if Nate and Naomi know of a Sam Taylor.
RYDER:	Let me contact Nate and Naomi.
MOLLY:	I'll rush over now.
RYDER:	You stay here and keep Liza company. I'll go over.
MOLLY:	Liza and I have all night to get acquainted. If you'll excuse me please . . .

RYDER: Molly!

Molly stops and turns to Ryder—speaking with trepidation.

MOLLY: Something the matter?
RYDER: I'm fine dear. I wanted—

                    (*Grabbing invitation from table*)

                    I wanted to give you Nate's and Naomi's invitation
                    to the ball.
MOLLY: Oh, thanks.

                    (*With uneasy relief*)

                    They'll be delighted. I'll return shortly.

Ryder watches Molly leave. As she is moving out of sight, he calls out in panic.

RYDER: Molly!

Molly stops and turns, uneasily.

MOLLY: Yes?

Ryder takes Molly by the hand.

RYDER: Be sure to give Nate and Naomi my regards, and
                    tell them I look forward to having them over for
                    dinner—sometime in the not-too-distant future.

Ryder plants a reassuring kiss on her lips.

MOLLY: I can't wait to see the look on their faces when I
                    break the news to them.

Molly exits, with Ryder looking longingly after her.

LIZA: I doubt if Mr. Nate's gwine te be any help ta Miss Molly. I recognize Mr. Nate as de man who sent me ta you, Mr. Ryda.

An unsettled Ryder is taken aback.

RYDER: Nate sent you to me?

LIZA: Mr. Nate tells me you left Nawth Calina undah cova wid de Hestah clan.

RYDER: The Hestah clan—what Nate tell you about the Hester clan?

LIZA: Oh, I's been knowin' 'bout de Hestah clan since befo de wa. Ya see, dey wuz free coloreds gwine Nawth. Dey tell me some of dem was so fair dat when dey got beyond de Mason and Dixon line, they crossed ovah de color line wid the white folk. I wuz told dey sneaked out slaves wid um. Dey's leaving Nawth Calina 'bout de time Sam escaped, but de ones who came back aftah de wa claimed dey nevah hud tell of Sam. 'Course Sam wuzn't de kind of man ta deny his roots.

RYDER: When it's life and death, ma'am, you do what it takes to stay alive.

LIZA: Now, if Sam was on dat Hestah train, he'd about changed his name.

RYDER: Everybody in the Hester clan was a Hester until they got to their northern destination.

LIZA: You reckon Sam went back ta being Sam Taylor after he parted with the Hestahs?

                         (*Noticing Ryder doesn't answer*)

                         You reckon Sam went back to being Sam Taylor, Mr. Ryder?

RYDER: Sam did what he had to do to survive, Liza.

LIZA: I's wonderin' how you managed ta git reunited wid your kinfolk aftah da wa. You go back ta Nawth Calina to see if you could hook up wid your folk afta de wa?

RYDER:	I couldn't—couldn't find them.
LIZA:	I's prayin' ta de Lawd Sam'd come back to Raleigh to git me aftah de wa, but I don't reckon he bothered ta come back.
RYDER:	Sam went back.
LIZA:	You reckon?
RYDER:	It was the proper thing for a man to do.
LIZA:	I don't know, Mr. Ryder.
RYDER:	Sam went back!
LIZA:	Sam ain't gave up on me?
RYDER:	He didn't know where else to go after Raleigh. He headed north where he had his home and his work. You should have come north when you didn't find Sam in Raleigh. You never should have wasted your life looking for Sam down south!
LIZA:	You's right, Mr. Ryda.
RYDER:	Why Charleston, for heaven's sake! Charleston is south of Raleigh! And New Orleans! New Orleans is at the end of the Mississippi River! You should have come north.
LIZA:	I should have come nawth a long time ago.
RYDER:	A long time ago, Liza!
LIZA:	You reckon I's too late gittin' heah?
RYDER:	Liza, you came as early as you could.
LIZA:	I know twenty-five years is a long time, but do you think Sam'd be able ta recognize me if he's ta se me?
RYDER:	Sam's memory probably faded.
LIZA:	Sam's memory ain't faded!
RYDER:	A man's memory fades!
LIZA:	Love don't fade, Mr. Ryder! Never, Mr. Ryder!
RYDER:	Listen, Liza . . .
LIZA:	Ain't dat de way it's supposed to be?
RYDER:	Nothing is the way it's supposed to be anymore, Liza!
LIZA:	I reckon you's right. Sam bout don't know who de devil I is no mo'. You must think I done gone crazy as a loon, me standing here lookin' at you calling out Sam Taylor when I'm supposed to be sayin' Mr. Ryda.

(After a moment, Ryder doesn't respond)

Ain't thought about no life widout Sam. We always wanted a fine home of our own and heap ov chullun. I's beyond that stage now, but I's hopin' we'd get together in time to make somethin' out de few good yeahs de Lawd left fer us.

A tormented Ryder struggles to respond.

RYDER:	Liza . . .
LIZA:	Sometimes I git kind weary and falters, but I git a second wind and I goes on 'cause I know my Sam's waitin' fer me.
RYDER:	Liza. It's going to be very painful for Sam to recognize the wife of his youth if his heart is set on another woman.
LIZA:	Sam's heart ain't set on another woman!
RYDER:	Don't you remember why Sam escaped from old man Womack's plantation?
LIZA:	Yeah—so we'd be together in freedom.
RYDER:	To be together in freedom! But the only way Sam could be with you was to run away. Old Man Womack was putting Sam on the auction block the next day and that was to be the end of Sam and Liza!
LIZA:	Dat's why me and Sam made our git away plans under dat old hickory tree.
RYDER:	The minute Sam said good-bye under that old hickory tree and ran for his life he was a fugitive slave, not a *free man*. Stealing back onto Old Man Womack's plantation and escaping to freedom to live happily ever after with Liza was a fantasy. The real world was ducking and dodging bloodhounds, outwitting the posse, dashing through the woods like a bat out of hell so the water moccasins and rattlesnakes couldn't strike his heels! Living in the woods among wild animals by day and stealing his way down the roads by night! Liza, maybe things

	would have worked out better if you'd let Old Man Womack sell Sam down the river!
LIZA:	Sam wud die befo' he let Massa Womack sell him down de river.
RYDER:	Died, Liza. Sam would have died before he let his daddy put him on that auction block and separate him from the woman he loved.
LIZA:	I wud a died wid um!
RYDER:	Died! Died is what Sam did when he escaped Old Man Womack's plantation.
LIZA:	Sam ain't dead!
RYDER:	Sam Taylor is dead, Liza!
LIZA:	*My Sam ain't dead!*
RYDER:	Liza, listen to me. You know what Willie Hester did? He took Sam Taylor aboard his wagon and gave him the name of his dead son—Eli Hester. A dead man's name was his lot as a fugitive slave. When he did that, Sam Taylor died.
LIZA:	No!
RYDER:	Yes!
LIZA:	I told ya. Sam ain't dead.
RYDER:	Dead, Liza!
LIZA:	I ain't gonna let you bury my Sam.
RYDER:	Listen to me. Liza, Sam went back to Raleigh—folk in Raleigh said go to Charleston. Folk in Charleston said go back to Raleigh.
LIZA:	I's headed ta New Oiluns . . .
RYDER:	The day Sam started loading them suitcases at Ohio Central, he was thinking of Liza. He started laying plans for the dream house for her and the children they were going to have to fill it with life. Can you hear the floors rumbling with the sounds of our children ripping and running through the halls? I can hear those empty bedrooms filled with kids laughing and playing. Can you hear them?
LIZA:	Sam?

Ryder explodes in anger.

RYDER:	Look at what Sam built for Liza. For you, Liza!
LIZA:	Me?

Ryder reacts with bitter contempt and anger.

RYDER:	Where the hell were you, woman?
LIZA:	Sam?
RYDER:	Dammit, you've ruined me!
LIZA:	Lawd today. My Sam!
RYDER:	Why the hell did you come back now? Today was perfect! You've ruined me! You! Coming back out of the past like a ghost rising out of the grave. Your beat-up bags, tattered plantation rags on your back! After all these years! Say something—don't stand there like a knot on a log! God Woman! Why didn't you die and rot in your grave with Old Man Womack!

(*Shocked, ashamed at the gravity of his accusation, Ryder drops to his knees in contrition.*)

Jesus! Dear God, if you're in heaven above, reach down here this second and strike your servant dead—banish him to burn in eternal hell fire for wishing death on the woman he once held in his arms under that old hickory tree.

(*Turning to Liza, pleading*)

Say something to me. Say something to me! Tell Josh Ryder to die and burn in hell! Tell him, Liza! *Tell him!*

After a moment of unbearably painful silence, Liza speaks.

LIZA:	Last time I's in Raleigh, dat old hickory tree wuz still standin'.
RYDER:	Sam and . . . Liza.
LIZA:	It wuz callin' fer me and Sam.

RYDER: Sam and Liza used to sneak out and get together under that hickory tree—make a bed of fresh wild flowers, then they'd settle down in each other's arms. Remember the silvery moonlight under the hickory tree the night before Sam left? It was a beautiful Indian summer. The ground was a bed of golden leaves. They sprawled their cotton sacks on the leaves and lay down on the sacks, except they had to get up because burlap kept itching your back. So they sneaked out in the cotton fields and picked cotton and covered the burlap with a soft pallet of cotton. God, it was quiet and soft under the moonlight. Remember?

(*As Liza nods affirmatively*)

The bullfrogs and crickets playing our song.

Liza responds with muted laughter.

LIZA: 'Twas kind a bumpy.
RYDER: God knows it was bumpy.
LIZA: Until we got de bed of cotton down.
RYDER: Then Sam reached beneath your shoulders and clasped his hands together beneath your back until he felt your hard nipples tickling his chest, your hot breath singing in his ears. And he pulled you close. Sam and Liza close, so close until their pounding hearts became one.
LIZA: We wuz nippin' each otha's lips ta smutha our moaning.
RYDER: Then at the moment of—when Sam was—just as the stars were exploding that blasted hickory nut fell from the tree and the stem popped Sam right in his left rear cheek.

They share a moment of tender, mutual laughter. Liza responds through tearful laughter and teasing.

LIZA:	Old Sam thought a Nawth Calina rattlesnake had clamped his fangs into his butt!
RYDER:	Sam's old black behind itched for years and years!
LIZA:	Mercy me!

The infectious laughter crescendos and begins dying.

RYDER:	Sam would have been hanged, quartered, and burned before he let Old Man Womack auction him off from his Liza.
LIZA:	Sam brought me a bouquet of Rose of Sharon.

Ryder can't resist a moment of muted laughter at his mischief.

RYDER:	Sneaked them out of Massa Womack's garden.

They laugh at the memories. For an indescribably beautiful moment, the many years separating them are swept aside. Liza reaches out for Ryder, and he responds with a spasmodic embrace and passionate kiss.

LIZA:	Sam!
RYDER:	Liza!

Ryder begins a self-conscious, fearful retreat. It is one that disturbs and frightens them both.

LIZA:	Sam?
RYDER:	I'm Josh Ryder, Liza!
LIZA:	Lawd, today—my Sam Taylor don't know who he is no mo'. I's free, but I ain't forgot who I is.
RYDER:	Molly was my last chance to bring light into my life. Sam didn't have the power to stop Old Man Womack from coming between him and Liza, but Josh Ryder was determined to stop anything from coming between him and Molly Dixon!
LIZA:	Sam?
RYDER:	No, Liza—No, Liza.
LIZA:	Sam Taylor don't know who he is no mo'.
RYDER:	Liza . . .

Liza gathers her belongings.

LIZA:	Don't know who he is no mo'.
RYDER:	Where are you going?
LIZA:	Ta de train station.
RYDER:	No, Liza, I don't want you to go.
LIZA:	De train be comin' soon.
RYDER:	No.
LIZA:	Don't won't ta miss my train.
RYDER:	What about us?
LIZA:	I ain't got no use for a man who don't know who he is.
RYDER:	I'll help you find a place to stay here.
LIZA:	Be jes a house wid a roof on it widout Sam.

Molly enters unobserved. She still has the invitation in her hand.

RYDER:	I want you to stay, Liza!
LIZA:	De place I's lookin' fer is de one me and Sam had under dat hickory tree.

> (*Stopping and turning to Molly*)

I's thankful fer yo hospitality dis aftahnoon, Miss Molly.

Molly and Liza stare at each other for a brief moment, but Molly is unable to respond. As Liza makes her way to the exit, Ryder calls out to her.

RYDER:	Liza—I'm . . . I'm sorry about Miss Luella.
LIZA:	I thank ya fer helpin' me find Sam Taylor, Mr. Ryda.

Liza exits. Ryder crosses to Molly.

RYDER:	Molly.

A hurt Molly turns away.

MOLLY:	I don't even know who you are.
RYDER:	Sweetheart . . .
MOLLY:	I'm afraid I don't.
RYDER:	Don't say that.

Ryder reaches out for Molly, but she rejects his advance.

MOLLY:	Don't touch me!
RYDER:	You must hear me out.
MOLLY:	Why didn't you tell me Nate Williams is the man who risked his life and family to secure your freedom? And you don't think they're good enough for your society?
RYDER:	I suppose he told you about Naomi too.
MOLLY:	God, Josh, his family disowned him and made him change his birth name from Willie Hester because he married a slave girl. She wasn't good enough to inherit the family name! Wasn't it awful enough for Nate's family to shun him?
RYDER:	Look at me.
MOLLY:	How could you?
RYDER:	What would you have done if you had known the truth about my past?

(*Molly turns away.*)

What if you had known that Josh Ryder had never set foot in a schoolhouse? Would he have been good enough for Molly Dixon with her Howard University degree and your—

Rider halts.

MOLLY:	Say it, Josh!
RYDER:	No, I can't.
MOLLY:	It won't wash off if you say it!
JOSH:	Molly!
MOLLY:	Look at yourself. You don't even qualify for the society that you've come to lead.

RYDER:	You're right, Molly. They didn't want me anymore than they wanted Charlie Reid. Josh Ryder was nobody until this house became the pride of Groveland. Then they wanted me in the society.
MOLLY:	And you said yes.
RYDER:	I said yes to the society because it was the best place in the world to hide. Look at me. I've spent my life running and running and hiding—and waiting and waiting. Waiting for someone until I gave her up for dead! And then you came along. Don't make me wait any longer, Molly. You know the truth about my past.
MOLLY:	It's not your past I'm ashamed of. It's what you have become that frightens me.
RYDER:	I said yes to the free birth rule because I wanted to get closer to you. It's what I thought you wanted.
MOLLY:	You thought I wanted?
RYDER:	Yes.
MOLLY:	No, it's not what I wanted.
RYDER:	Molly . . .
MOLLY:	You can strike Nate and Naomi off the guest list for the ball.
RYDER:	No, I want Nate and Naomi to be at the ball with us.
MOLLY:	It's too late, Josh.
RYDER:	How can it be too late?

Molly hands Ryder back Nate's invitation.

MOLLY:	Nate turned down your invitation.

Molly starts for the door.

RYDER:	Molly!

Molly stops. After a painful moment, she turns to Ryder.

MOLLY:	I was the most honored woman in the world when Naomi introduced you to me that Sunday at the

church anniversary. You had a touch of greatness about you. A touch of greatness—the kind of quality every woman yearns to see in a man.

RYDER: There's nothing standing in our way now.
MOLLY: Nothing, Josh?
JOSH: Please understand me . . .
MOLLY: You dare say that to me now?
RYDER: You're all I have left in this world.
MOLLY: I must be on my way.

Molly has turned away to avoid acknowledging Ryder.

RYDER: Molly!
MOLLY: I have to go, Josh.
RYDER: No.
MOLLY: (*Through tears, torn*) Yes . . . I . . . I must go.
RYDER: No!
MOLLY: Josh!
RYDER: Molly!

Molly rushes out. Ryder stares at the flowers for a moment. Reaches in vase and grabs them along with hand full of invitations, turns toward the house, starts up the steps, as if the life is draining from his body. The flowers fall to the steps. After a moment, he rises, gets his hat, and walks resolutely in the direction the two women departed.

END OF PLAY

PAUL ROBESON PERFORMING ARTS COMPANY
BLUE VEIN SOCIETY
1988 PRODUCTION

The Blue Vein Society was first staged at the Paul Robeson Performing Art Company in December 1988 at Onondaga Community College in Syracuse, NY. The production included the following artists and production staff:

CAST

Kristn Diefendorf .... Molly
Elleen Hannah .... Liza
Chalton Witherspoon .... Josh Ryder

PRODUCTION STAFF

Director .... Charles Horne
Set Design .... Don Padgett
Costume Design .... Annette Adams-Brown
Stage Manager .... Darryl Mercer

PAUL ROBESON PERFORMING ARTS COMPANY OFFICERS

Executive Director.. William H. Rowland II
Artistic Director ....Roy Delemos
Director of Dramatic Ensemble.. Joseph Edwards
Administrative Assistant .... Fatimah Salaam
Program Development .... Saundra Smokes
Research Associate..Barbara Vojta
Musical Director ....Robert Hamilton
Company Artist.. Corry Lyons
Vocal Coach .... Mary Gauthier
Marketing Assistant.. Michelle Walker

"Samuel Kelley's *The Blue Vein Society* is an example of the surge of play
scripts springing up around the country that display the psychological,
social, economic, and political conditions that continue to plague African
Americans today. Black America has a story to tell, and no one can tell the
story better than we can. The African American experience is unique while
at the same time appreciated for its universal human qualities."

—William H. Rowland II
Executive Director, Paul Robeson Performing Arts Company
November 1988

BACKGROUND AND
PRODUCTION HISTORY

Blue Vein Society was developed in the Drama 50 playwriting workshop at the Yale School of Drama. It is based on "The Wife of His Youth," a short story by the eminent nineteenth-century author Charles Chesnutt, the first African American fiction writer to achieve international prominence. *Blue Vein Society* is *not* an adaptation, but a play in its own right. It is requested that producing theaters and companies acknowledge Chesnutt's story. It is one way to bring recognition to African American authors who continue to languish in obscurity.

In addition to the Drama 50 production at Yale, *Blue Vein Society* has received numerous productions. These include the State University of New York College, the Paul Robeson Performing Arts Company at Syracuse University, the Yale School of Drama Cabaret Theatre, the *National Association of Speech and Dramatic Arts Festival*, Florida A & M University, Columbia College in Chicago, and Spelman College in Atlanta, Georgia. Other productions include the *Juneteenth Festival* in June 1997 at the University of Louisville, *Juneteenth Legacy Theatre*, Louisville, Kentucky, fall 2000 and February 2001. Additional productions include University of Louisville 2002 Juneteenth Festival, Global Short Story Conference in New Orleans, Louisiana (July 1998), and Strolling Players in Albuquerque, New Mexico (February 1998). Syracuse University brought the production back in the fall of 2008 to celebrate a twenty-year revival. The overwhelmingly positive response has been unanimous since it first appeared at the Yale school of Drama as a workshop production. It remains popular with audiences across race, gender, and age, and is particularly popular with high school students—as was shown in Albuquerque, New Mexico, when the high school students joined in to assist with the production and served as the first audience for that production.

This publication makes this work available to theatres and individuals at all levels—professional, community, schools and colleges—who are seeking to produce works of historical and social significance.

NO HIDIN' PLACE

"I presume that hanging might be pleasant if a man could only convince himself that it would not be painful, nor disgraceful, nor terminate his earthly career."

—Charles Waddell Chesnutt

NO HIDIN' PLACE

SETTING: Branson County, North Carolina
Post Reconstruction
Exterior of Sheriff Franklin's home
Branson County Jail

THE CAST

Sheriff Franklin .... County Sheriff; mid-fifties
Tom ....Franklin's mulatto son; thirty
Polly... Franklin's daughter, late twenties
Deputy Hoyden .... deputy sheriff; mid-forties

Scene One

Exterior of Sheriff Franklin's home.

Deputy Hoyden is angry and not very sober as he talks to Sheriff Franklin.

HOYDEN: It's a awful sight to see Captain Walker lying on a concrete slab wid stab wounds piercing his beloved heart. God-awful! Never a day went by that I didn't slow down to git my blessing from Captain. He's the biggest hero ta ever come out of Branson County.

FRANKLIN: No doubt about it. He served his country with honor and valor.

HOYDEN:	He did better than that. He left his right arm on the battlefield fighting Yankees at Gettysburg. Now he's foully murdered. Ain't no hidin' place on God's earth for the nigger mulatto who murdered Captain Walker.
FRANKLIN:	We can't be so certain of the murderer.
HOYDEN:	I wanna know whether or not you calling into question the judgment of the citizens of Branson County?
FRANKLIN:	Did anyone you know see the nigger going or leaving Captain Walker's?
HOYDEN:	Ezra Kingstead passed a mulatto fleeing Captain Walker's place on his way to town.
FRANKLIN:	Ezra didn't place him at the scene of the crime.
HOYDEN:	How much closer did Ezra need to be? Doc Caine swears he met up with a mulatto on his way from delivering Missy Holder's new baby. A nigger mulatto was seen going in the direction of Captain Walker's house Thursday night. That's three sightings. Got to be the same nigger.
FRANKLIN:	Nobody has placed him at the scene of the crime.
HOYDEN:	Ain't but two main roads can carry a man out of town. We gotta bring the nigger in before he escapes across the county line. I got a dozen men saddled up and ready to hit the road.
FRANKLIN:	No need for that.
HOYDEN:	You never hesitated with a nigger before. How come you doing so now?
FRANKLIN:	I brought the suspect in while Branson County slept last night.
HOYDEN:	Well, I'll be damned. Judge Bingham said he had a hunch that might be the case. How come we just now hearing of it?
FRANKLIN:	You know me. I like to stay a step ahead of the crowd.
HOYDEN:	The citizens done met, and we've decided to meet out justice to fit the crime. Hanging is too good for Captain Walker's murderer.

FRANKLIN:	You don't want to usurp the power of Judge Bingham.
HOYDEN:	Judge Bingham taken sick with the flu. He can't hold court this afternoon.
FRANKLIN:	He'll be recovered enough to hold the preliminary hearing next week.
HOYDEN:	Ain't nobody waiting that long. This here is the meanest darn murder ever committed in Branson County. That lowlife is gonna burn at the stake.
FRANKLIN:	Careful, you don't want to create a martyr of a nigger, do you now?

Hoyden takes several swallows from a bottle of moonshine whiskey.

HOYDEN:	You gonna stand by and let a worthless nigger kill the best white man in Branson County?
FRANKLIN:	Any reason why the prisoner would kill Captain Walker?
HOYDEN:	I see this town needs somebody who's gonna represent the wishes of the citizens.
FRANKLIN:	Hoyden, are you planning on running for sheriff?
HOYDEN:	I'll tell you what the good citizens done decided on.
FRANKLIN:	What might that be?
HOYDEN:	A midnight picnic. Last time we held a midnight picnic was when the Wells nigger winked at Sarah Stuart. Lynching that mulatto over a bed of coals is the only fitting way to honor Captain's memory.
FRANKLIN:	Let me remind you that no citizen is above the law.
HOYDEN:	A nigger killed a white man. He's gonna burn. The citizens are meeting as we speak.
FRANKLIN:	You mean the *lynching* party is meeting.
HOYDEN:	What's that?
FRANKLIN:	The lynching party met twice last night.

Hoyden is taken aback to hear that Franklin is aware of the meeting.

HOYDEN:	Who told you?

FRANKLIN:	It's my duty to know. Right, Hoyden?
HOYDEN:	You telling me or not?
FRANKLIN:	Tell your men they'll have to lynch the Branson County Sheriff before they get to the prisoner. Any citizen caught violating the law will be subject to the same punishment as the prisoner.
HOYDEN:	Sheriff, every white man in Branson County knows you was for the Union Army. You went way too far north to get your college degree.
FRANKLIN:	I don't consider Raleigh, North Carolina, so far north.
HOYDEN:	Plenty folk in Branson County do.
FRANKLIN:	Every man in Branson County knows I fought with the Confederate Army and served with distinction through three campaigns.
HOYDEN:	You joined up with the Confederate Army when popular opinion turned against ya.
FRANKLIN:	Come now, Hoyden, I can count the Branson County men who served in the war on both hands and still have about eight fingers to spare. Did you forget? You turned into an Indian chief yourself.
HOYDEN:	Where you hear that?
FRANKLIN:	Are you denying that you suddenly turned into some kind of Indian chief? As I said before, being in the know is my job. As for the mob, I'm counting on you to carry out your duties as deputy sheriff. Go on now.

Hoyden hesitates and then goes off in a huff. Entering on his heels, practically out of breath, is Polly Franklin, a woman in her mid-twenties. She is very protective of her father.

POLLY:	Papa, Branson Square is filled with outraged citizens. The mob is certain to lynch the prisoner tonight.
FRANKLIN:	Who's leading the mob?
POLLY:	Doc Caine and Colonel Higgins. Two of the most upright citizens in Bransonville! They say Captain Walker kept two barrels of confederate money

	around. Maybe the prisoner was trying to steal the money.
FRANKLIN:	Why would the prisoner murder Captain Walker over useless money?
POLLY:	Perhaps he didn't know the difference.
FRANKLIN:	Are you sure you aren't appointed to the lynching committee?
POLLY:	Must you humiliate me?
FRANKLIN:	Forgive me. Who else is leading this charge?
POLLY:	Doc Caine, Colonel Higgins, Major McDonald. There are so many until I can't remember them all. Clara has prepared your dinner if you wish to eat.
FRANKLIN:	No thanks. No time for supper. I must get to the jail.
POLLY:	There is not a shred of reason left in the mob. I fear they'll shoot you if you don't give up the prisoner.
FRANKLIN:	All the more reason for me to stand up to them.
POLLY:	Must you put yourself at risk for a stranger who isn't even a citizen of Branson County?
FRANKLIN:	There isn't a man in Branson County in his right mind that would dare raise his gun to me.
POLLY:	Deputy Hoyden is a very dangerous man.
FRANKLIN:	Hoyden is a midget of a man.
POLLY:	Please, Father.
FRANKLIN:	As for Hoyden being dangerous, well . . .
POLLY:	You are the only relative I have left in this world.
FRANKLIN:	I've faced fire much too often to be frightened away from my duty by the likes of Hoyden.
POLLY:	I'm going to the jail with you.
FRANKLIN:	No, Polly. I won't permit it.
POLLY:	Did you forget? I held my own while you were away at the war.
FRANKLIN:	I know what you are capable of doing.
POLLY:	Then you'll take me with you?
FRANKLIN:	You must keep close to the house.
POLLY:	Please? I beg you!

Franklin passes pistol to Polly. Hoyden sneaks up and listens in on conversation, unseen by Polly and Franklin.

FRANKLIN:	If anyone disturbs you, here is the horse pistol. I know it's old-fashioned, but it will send a pack of hungry wolves scrambling. Stand watch while I get my firepower.
POLLY:	You don't think anyone would be so bold as to come here, do you?
FRANKLIN:	I put nothing past Hoyden. Should something go wrong and you were harmed at the jail, I could never forgive myself.

Hoyden darts away, still unseen. Franklin enters the house while an anxious Polly stands watch. He quickly returns with a shotgun.

POLLY:	Promise me you'll do nothing to put yourself in harm's way.
FRANKLIN:	I promise to uphold the law to the best of my ability. If that places me in harm's way, so be it.

Polly embraces her father.

POLLY:	I have no one to look after me except you.
FRANKLIN:	If you hear a shot fired . . .
POLLY:	No!

Polly clings to her father.

FRANKLIN:	God be with you, my dear daughter.
POLLY:	You mustn't say that! I shall be on guard for any strange noise from there.
FRANKLIN:	Consider every white man who comes to the house tonight a stranger. No one is allowed inside. Polly, everything I own is in your name.
POLLY:	Please! You're my father, but I forbid you to speak in that tone. Papa . . .

Franklin exits quickly. Polly takes a few longing steps in his direction. Hoyden sneaks in on the periphery, watching. Polly enters the house. Hoyden looks around until he is certain that Franklin is safely out of sight. He tiptoes forward and calls Polly's name.

HOYDEN: Miss Franklin?

Polly enters. She is visibly unnerved by Hoyden's sudden appearance, but tries to collect herself.

POLLY: Why, Deputy Hoyden! I wasn't expecting to see you. I presume you are looking for Sheriff Franklin. Just this minute he left for the jail.
HOYDEN: Oh?
POLLY: You should have passed him on your way here. He took Quail Road. Rush on now. You'll catch up to him.
HOYDEN: I wasn't trying to catch up with the sheriff, Miss Polly.
POLLY: I beg your pardon?
HOYDEN: No, ma'am.
POLLY: May I inquire as to your business here?
HOYDEN: I've come for the keys to the jail.
POLLY: Sheriff Franklin has the keys with him.
HOYDEN: Sheriff keeps a second pair at home.
POLLY: Oh, I'm afraid I don't recall where they are.
HOYDEN: They in the pantry.
POLLY: Oh, yes, in the pantry.
HOYDEN: I'll have a look, if you don't mind.
POLLY: No thanks. I'll check. Wait here, please.

Polly goes into the house, cautiously, glancing back at Hoyden as she goes inside. Hoyden waits outside, annoyed at having been bested. He shouts to Polly.

HOYDEN: They hang in the right-hand corner below the pickled cucumbers!
POLLY: I'm looking.
HOYDEN: That's where I saw them last!

Hoyden looks around cautiously, curiously. Polly returns.

POLLY: I'm afraid we're out of luck.
HOYDEN: That can't be.
POLLY: I do believe Papa has taken both sets with him.

HOYDEN: Sheriff never takes both sets.

POLLY: Well, it certainly appears he did this time.

HOYDEN: You sure about that?

POLLY: Deputy Hoyden, what need have you for another set of keys, if you don't mind my asking? The prisoner is secure with Father.

HOYDEN: We ain't so certain about that. Mind if I have a look for the keys myself?

POLLY: You'll have to speak with Sheriff Franklin if you have further need for the keys. I'm sure you'll catch up to him if you rush on now.

HOYDEN: Miss Polly?

POLLY: Yes?

HOYDEN: There's much concern about Sheriff going ta such great lengths to protect a murderer.

POLLY: Deputy Hoyden, Papa goes to great lengths to protect every *prisoner* in his charge.

HOYDEN: He ain't never gone to such lengths before to protect a nigger prisoner.

POLLY: It is his duty to uphold the law, regardless of the race of the prisoner. I'm sure you would agree with that.

HOYDEN: This ain't no ordinary prisoner Sheriff Franklin is protecting.

POLLY: I'm not sure I understand.

HOYDEN: I don't know as I expect you to understand such matters.

POLLY: What makes the prisoner extraordinary as you claim?

HOYDEN: I take it you haven't seen the prisoner.

POLLY: Should I have seen him?

HOYDEN: The prisoner was seen fleeing Captain Walker's about the time he was murdered.

POLLY: That much I have heard, Deputy Hoyden.

HOYDEN: Good!

POLLY: What does this have to do with Papa?

HOYDEN: A search of the young man's background turned up a Cicely Franklin as his mother.

POLLY: Perhaps you should be more direct, Deputy Hoyden. I'm afraid that I'm still in the dark.

HOYDEN:	Well, Cicely was a fourteen-year-old household servant of your daddy's. It seems to me there is a conflict of interest, if you know what I mean.

Polly realizes where Hoyden is headed.

POLLY:	How dare you blaspheme my father with your despicable lies!
HOYDEN:	Miss Polly, our Southern belles ain't often privy to the seamier side of their heritage.
POLLY:	Deputy Hoyden! You will leave these premises this minute!
HOYDEN:	Miss Polly . . .
POLLY:	You are too inebriated to know of what you speak. Please be on your way.

Polly stands her ground. Hoyden storms off in a huff. Lights down.

Scene Two

The jail cell. The crowd is increasingly loud and unruly. Franklin matches them in a booming voice of a man who remains steadfast and unmovable.

FRANKLIN:	I don't know what business you all have here at the jail! I've apprehended the prisoner! As far as I am concerned, you are all strangers to me.
	(*The angry voices rise louder.*)
	Don't speak all at once! You're taxing my ears! Send in the head spokesman!

Hoyden walks forward.

HOYDEN:	As you requested, sheriff.
FRANKLIN:	Just as I suspected, you're the leader of the esteemed lynching committee.
HOYDEN:	The citizens demand access to the jail.

FRANKLIN:	Not much trouble getting into jail. Most people want to keep out.
HOYDEN:	We wanna talk with the nigger prisoner that killed Captain Walker.
FRANKLIN:	You're free to talk to the prisoner when he's brought up for trial.
HOYDEN:	We ain't waiting that long.

Franklin shouts to the crowd, trying to be a bit humorous, but it isn't working.

FRANKLIN:	Do you good citizens want to take the bread out of a poor man's mouth? I get seventy-five cents a day for keeping this prisoner. He's the only one in jail! I can't have my family suffer on account of a lynch mob.
HOYDEN:	We'll pay you that ten times over. The lynching is gonna be the main picnic attraction. You'll more than recoup your loss.
FRANKLIN:	You'll have no picnic over my prisoner's body I know my duty and I mean to uphold it to the fullest of my ability.
HOYDEN:	No white man and his family will be safe in this town if we don't teach the niggers they place.
FRANKLIN:	I'm not surrendering this jail as long as I'm able to pull the trigger on this double-barrel shotgun.
HOYDEN:	We'll bust the door open if we have to.
FRANKLIN:	The first man that tries to bust open my door will be filled with buckshot. I'm blasting you first, Hoyden. Tell your lynching committee to get moving away from here.
HOYDEN:	You don't stand a chance.
FRANKLIN:	I've faced fire before with nothing between the enemy and me. Move the hell out of here. Now!
HOYDEN:	I'm moving, but I'm telling you right now. We ain't canceling the picnic.

Hoyden reluctantly moves out. Franklin closes window and turns to the prisoner. The latter is crouched in the corner.

TOM:	For God's sake, don't let them lynch me.
FRANKLIN:	Get up!
TOM:	I didn't kill that old man.
FRANKLIN:	You are going to hang. I'll see to it, but it won't be tonight if I can help it.
TOM:	These fetters are hurting my hand. Please, can you loosen them up? I'd appreciate it.
FRANKLIN:	Be thankful you aren't dead. The mob wants justice for your heinous crime.
TOM:	You must hear me out. I didn't kill that old man.
FRANKLIN:	One more word out of you and the mob won't have to lynch you.
TOM:	I didn't kill him!
FRANKLIN:	Quiet! I'm going to unlock your fetters, but not for the reason you think.
TOM:	You're going to release me to the mob!
FRANKLIN:	I'm more of a man than that. Listen up. If I can't hold the mob back, you'll have to put up the best fight you can. You got that?
TOM:	Yes, sir, Sheriff.

Tom starts to the window to have a peek.

FRANKLIN:	Keep back from the window! I'm going to do my best to keep the mob away, but don't take that as a sign of pity for nigger murderers. You're lucky only a handful of the mob came. We'd both be dead if the whole lot of them had come prepared to take you by force.

(*Shouting to crowd*)

Move on out! |

The crowd is heard departing. Franklin removes his revolver and lays it on the bench. Then he takes his stand with the side of the window where he can see outside with the least exposure.

TOM:	They go yet, sir?
FRANKLIN:	Hoyden is holding council on his next move. I dare not turn my back on a traitor. Besides, he reeks with Carson's moonshine. It's hard to tell which is doing the talking.
TOM:	Do you think they'll run us over?
FRANKLIN:	No one out there wants to follow Captain Walker just yet.
TOM:	What if they come?
FRANKLIN:	Quiet! I can't watch in both directions at the same time.

A shot is fired from the outside. Franklin ducks. The bullet lodges in the wooden casing a few inches from Franklin. He fires twice in the direction of the mob, and it scatters. Hoyden rushes up.

HOYDEN:	Don't shoot!
FRANKLIN:	I told you to move out!
HOYDEN:	All right, all right. The committee done called off our plans for the time being. They want me to stand guard.
FRANKLIN:	I'm not so foolish as to leave the fox to guard the chicken coup.

         (*Chuckling lightly*)

         Don't worry. The prisoner won't be escaping any time tonight.

Tom crawls, stealthily, to Franklin's bench and eases the sheriff's pistol from the bench and rushes back to his corner.

HOYDEN:	I'm going to put it straight to ya, Sheriff. We don't think you the one to guard the prisoner. I believe you do know the reason why.
FRANKLIN:	Maybe. You want to tell me to my face?

Hoyden hesitates. Then he speaks.

| HOYDEN: | A man who'd kill the biggest hero in Branson County oughtn't to be left alone with one guard. |
| FRANKLIN: | I'm telling you for the last time. |

Franklin raises gun as if prepared to shoot.

HOYDEN:	No need for that, Sheriff.
FRANKLIN:	Tell your men there will be no Branson County picnic tonight.
HOYDEN:	I'm going, but I'll be back.

Hoyden marches off. Franklin stares in Hoyden's direction, poised for trouble for a moment. Then he turns, instinctively, for his pistol only to find himself staring down the barrel of his own revolver. Tom's eyes glisten with rage.

| TOM: | Stay where you are. |

A stunned Franklin struggles to project a calm air.

FRANKLIN:	You don't want to do anything rash.
TOM:	Shut up!
FRANKLIN:	Calm down now.
TOM:	It was a stupid mistake to place your gun where I could gain access to it.
FRANKLIN:	I trusted you.

Tom chuckles bitterly.

TOM:	You trusted a colored prisoner accused of murder?
FRANKLIN:	I have to look out for both of us.
TOM:	No such thing. You were relying on the Negro's cowardice and subordination in the presence of an armed white man. You expected me to stay crouched in that corner, sweating in fear and panic. That was your mistake.

The two men engage in a fearsome duel with their eyes, neither one blinking. Franklin blinks.

FRANKLIN:	What do you aim to do?
TOM:	I'm going to plot my escape from this hellhole.
FRANKLIN:	Every white man, woman, and child in Branson County has a license to kill you.
TOM:	And not one of them needs a license to lynch me.
FRANKLIN:	One minute ago, you were a groveling wretch crouched in the corner, begging for your life.
TOM:	That made you feel superior enough to place a pistol in my reach and turn your back on me. Do you know why?
FRANKLIN:	Why?
TOM:	You did so because I didn't exist to you.
FRANKLIN:	You're not from around here, are you?
TOM:	Why do you ask?
FRANKLIN:	You speak better than any man I know in Branson County. You have a respectable level of education.
TOM:	That I have, but no thanks to you. There isn't so much as a single room schoolhouse to educate the colored man in Branson County.
FRANKLIN:	Show some gratitude. If I hadn't fought off the mob, you'd be hanging from a tree.

Tom spurts a bitter chuckle.

TOM:	You held them off, but for how long? I'll hang from a tree.
FRANKLIN:	You can prove your innocence.
TOM:	Prove my innocence to a mob that is my judge, jury, and executioner? I didn't kill the old man, but I shall never be able to clear myself.
FRANKLIN:	You were at Captain Walker's house.
TOM:	How do you know?
FRANKLIN:	You were wearing Captain Walker's coat on your back when I captured you?
TOM:	I was there at nine o'clock. Yes, I snatched his coat to have something to keep me warm for the chilly night.
FRANKLIN:	That doesn't account for the confederate money in your jacket.

TOM:	That useless money was already in the jacket. I didn't go upstairs. I ran away at the sound of a prowler.
FRANKLIN:	Who was there?
TOM:	I was too busy running away to check. The only thing I saw was his outline in the room upstairs where you claim they found the captain.
FRANKLIN:	Hoyden?
TOM:	Maybe, maybe not. You'll have to ask him that.
FRANKLIN:	You want to give the judge an alibi? Then you'd better find someone who can place you far away from Captain Walker's at the time of his death. The mob wants revenge the fastest way they can get it.
TOM:	If you keep them away until the verdict comes down at the trial, you are the man who will lead the hanging, right?
FRANKLIN:	I am that man if the verdict is guilty.
TOM:	So it is merely a choice between two ropes: sooner by the mob, or later by Sheriff Franklin.
FRANKLIN:	Looks that way.

Tom raises his gun with resolve.

TOM:	Look again. I will not hang. Throw me the keys.
FRANKLIN:	I'll burn in hell before I hand these keys to a nigger murderer.
TOM:	You frightened off the posse, but I have nothing to fear.
FRANKLIN:	Not even death itself?
TOM:	Sheriff, you mean you don't know why?
FRANKLIN:	You'll have to enlighten me.
TOM:	Hand over the keys.
FRANKLIN:	Can't do that.
TOM:	Ten seconds—if the keys are in your hands, I shall turn this cell into a grave for the both of us. Ten, nine, eight, seven, six, five, four, three, two, one.

Franklin flings keys against Tom's chest, hoping to throw him off guard, but Tom throws them back.

FRANKLIN: You don't know what you're getting into.
TOM: Shut up!
FRANKLIN: Hear me out . . .
TOM: Quiet! If you make one false move, you'll sleep next
                   to Captain Walker. Now, throw the keys back to
                   me as a respectable gentleman should.

Franklin throws keys, this time with a gesture of conciliation.

FRANKLIN: Now what?
TOM: Thanks, Sheriff.
FRANKLIN: How far do you expect to get?
TOM: As far as I came—Washington, DC.
FRANKLIN: There are only two roads out of this county.
TOM: I know.
FRANKLIN: And you expect to escape?
TOM: I've got the nose of a bloodhound.

Franklin speaks through an uncomfortable laughter.

FRANKLIN: You've got the nose of a bloodhound.
TOM: Don't laugh. I found you, didn't I?

Tom throws keys to Franklin.

FRANKLIN: No.
TOM: Unlock the door.

Franklin hesitates. Tom doesn't blink.

FRANKLIN: No.
TOM: Do not second-guess me. Unlock the door.

Franklin blinks.

FRANKLIN: As you say. I'm opening the door.

Sheriff Franklin unlocks the door. He goes for the knob.

TOM:	Halt!
FRANKLIN:	I'm following your order.
TOM:	I said *unlock* the door. Now, get over in the corner where I was crouching like a coward of a man a few minutes ago.
FRANKLIN:	Stand, I shall. I crouch for no nigger.
TOM:	You will crouch when I say crouch. You will crawl when I say crawl. You will grovel when I say grovel.
FRANKLIN:	You've made your point.
TOM:	Shut up! I'll take my own life before I hang for a crime I didn't commit. But that would be foolish as long as I can save myself. In order to do that, I shall have to do something I've never done before. God help us both.
FRANKLIN:	It is a fool who would kill the very man to whom he owes his own life.
TOM:	You speak the truth—more than you truly know.
FRANKLIN:	Who are you?
TOM:	I am Tom, Cicely's son.

Cicely does not fully register with Frank at first, but something about the name strikes him.

FRANKLIN:	Cicely?
TOM:	Cicely . . .

(*Allowing it to sink in*)

The slave girl you sold to the speculator on his way to Alabama.

(*Franklin stares at Tom, curiously.*)

	She was sixteen when you put her on the auction block with her year-old son.
FRANKLIN:	I don't recall.

Tom removes his cap to reveal a striking resemblance to Franklin. He stares at Tom in speechless amazement.

TOM: Remember now? Same story—you had a year of bad crops, debts, and a helpless teenage mother and child were chosen to pay the price.

FRANKLIN: I kept a promise to see that you and your mother would be sold as a package.

TOM: And for that, I should be most grateful.

FRANKLIN: For an act committed so long ago, you would murder your own father?

TOM: What fatherly duties have you ever performed for me?

FRANKLIN: I gave you the life you cling to.

TOM: For that you dare utter the word *father* to me? You gave me a poor, wretched black mother. She was chattel that you sold to the highest bidder. And what are you to give me next? The lynch mob so that I may hang! Now you ask me to spare your life. You shame me.

FRANKLIN: Where is Cicely?

Tom's pain speaks louder than his anger as he responds to Franklin's question.

TOM: She dared to be woman enough to call her soul her own. For that, my poor mother died under the lash of a cruel slave master.

FRANKLIN: Sorry to hear of her fate. Are you Cicely's only child?

TOM: She bore two other children by men who treated her as chattel.

FRANKLIN: Then you do have family.

TOM: No, I do not. My mother had too much pride to let her children be raised under the yoke of a slave master who beat her each time she refused to submit to him. One day, she started talking in a strange tongue. My little brother and sister disappeared without warning. I inquired as to their whereabouts. Mama looked at me and wept. "My child, they crossed the River of Jordan under the watchful eyes of God."

Franklin doesn't speak for a painful moment.

FRANKLIN:	That is very unfortunate.
TOM:	It's heartbreaking.
FRANKLIN:	You are an educated man from the sound of your speech.
TOM:	I am. No thanks to my father.
SHERIFF:	What school?
TOM:	Howard University. What did I learn? I learned that no degree of learning or wisdom will change the color of my skin. It is badge of degradation with which I am cursed. As for Cicely, it will be no more than justice if I should avenge the wrongs inflicted upon my mother.
FRANKLIN:	There is enough of myself in you to make me believe you would never take another's life.
TOM:	Is there enough of you in me to make you believe that I am an innocent man?
FRANKLIN:	I wish I could say yes.
TOM:	Is there enough of you in me to make you believe I came searching for you to close one book in my life in order to open another?
FRANKLIN:	I'm in no position to say.
TOM:	You gave me your blood, your own features. For better or worse, for evil or good, you gave me a spirit as tough and resilient as your own. And now you are going to help your son escape.
FRANKLIN:	I can't do that.
TOM:	Then you leave me no choice but to take your life.
FRANKLIN:	Do what you have to do.
TOM:	Turn around.
FRANKLIN:	Only a coward would shoot a man in the back.
TOM:	You, who would oversee the hanging of your own flesh and blood, dare to call me a coward? God help you.
FRANKLIN:	I claim no fatherly duties to you.

TOM:	The words of a selfish coward. Turn around.
FRANKLIN:	You have no right to call me a coward!
TOM:	You would leave your daughter in this world alone, just like you left me and my mother.
FRANKLIN:	You will not accuse me of betraying Polly!
TOM:	It takes a real coward of a man to abandon his only daughter. Place your hands against the wall. Now! Legs wide apart.

Franklin obeys, reluctantly. Then he shouts.

FRANKLIN:	Wait!
TOM:	Coward!
FRANKLIN:	There is nothing I wouldn't do to save Polly. But I have a duty.
TOM:	To hang an innocent man! I won't allow you to carry out that duty.
FRANKLIN:	What is it you would have me do?
TOM:	Promise to give no alarm and make no attempt to capture me before daybreak.
FRANKLIN:	That I shall promise.
TOM:	You promised sixteen year-old Cicely that you wouldn't sell her, and when times grew hard, you sold her to the highest bidder. How do I know you won't scream or give some warning signal as soon as I am outside the door?
FRANKLIN:	You must trust me.
TOM:	Why should I trust you?
FRANKLIN:	I protected you from the mob.
TOM:	Only for a short while.
FRANKLIN:	I'm here now.
TOM:	Yes, but when the real showdown comes, will you be in here with me or out there with the mob?
FRANKLIN:	Look, I have unlocked the door. You are free to go.
TOM:	I want collateral.
FRANKLN:	You have my pistol. You can take my shotgun. Take whatever you want from me.

Franklin throws his watch and his knife to Tom.

TOM:	That's not enough.
FRANKLIN:	What more would you have from me, my life? I will open the door. You can walk away a free man.

Franklin walks, cautiously, toward the door. Tom begins to panic.

TOM:	Stop! You will not lead me into the hands of the lynch mob.
FRANKLIN:	I promise on my life. I will not lead you into the mob.
TOM:	No more broken promises! Turn around and face the wall.
FRANKLIN:	I beg you.
TOM:	There is only one way for me to walk free out of here.
FRANKLIN:	Please.
TOM:	You must give your life. It is my only way to freedom.

Tom raises his gun as if to shoot the sheriff. Polly enters, pistol drawn. Her hand trembles as she tries to fire it. Franklin sees her, but gives no hint.

FRANKLIN:	I beg of you, spare my life for the sake of Polly. I will do whatever it takes.
TOM:	Then you will lead me to your daughter. She'll come with me to the county line.
FRANKLIN:	I will lead you to my daughter. *Now*!

Polly fires pistol. It blasts the pistol from Tom's hand, injuring him. He is more stunned than wounded.

FRANKLIN:	Polly!
POLLY:	Papa!
FRANKLIN:	Stand guard!
POLLY:	Thank God I came.
FRANKLIN:	We must secure the prisoner.
POLLY:	I was just in time.

Franklin subdues and fetters Tom as quickly as possible.

FRANKLIN:	I'm glad it was you and not Hoyden.

Polly throws herself into her father's arms.

POLLY:	He was going to kill you!
FRANKLIN:	You're safe with your father. There, how quickly the tide of life changes.
POLLY:	I watched until Deputy Hoyden and his men went away. Then I followed close upon the heels of the last ones without being detected.
FRANKLIN:	What made you come?
POLLY:	The shots from the woods frightened me. I couldn't possibly stay home knowing you were in danger.
FRANKLIN:	You take after your father.
POLLY:	Deputy Hoyden came looking for the keys. What a wicked man! He threatened me in a most shameful manner.
FRANKLIN:	Hoyden threatened you? How so?
POLLY:	He dared to claim that you have a personal stake in protecting the prisoner.
FRANKLIN:	What is the nature of this personal stake?
POLLY:	I am too ashamed to utter the words.
FRANKLIN:	Polly, I must know in what manner Hoyden sought to shame you.
POLLY:	Papa, as I came up to the cell door, I overheard certain words spoken by the prisoner. Tell me it isn't so.
FRANKLIN:	I wish I could.
TOM:	You must tell her it isn't so.
FRANKLIN:	Quiet!
POLLY:	Father?

Tom removes his cap, uneasily.

TOM:	Look real close, Miss Polly.

Polly stares in quiet astonishment at the resemblance of Tom to her father.

FRANKLIN:	Ignore the prisoner.
POLLY:	How can I? Your youthful image stares at me as though it were a ghost from the past. What must we do when the men return tonight?
FRANKLIN:	They won't be back before dawn.
TOM:	They shall return.
POLLY:	Yes, Papa, they'll be back.
FRANKLIN:	Surely you're not listening to the prisoner.
POLLY:	I heard them. They'll return at midnight. We have very little time.
FRANKLIN:	Hoyden and his boys are making a terrible mistake. I captured the prisoner myself.
POLLY:	It means nothing to them. The mob plans to take the prisoner by force.
TOM:	I shall die for a crime I did not commit.

Polly stares, curiously, at Tom. She is torn as to what to make of the situation.

POLLY:	Is the prisoner deranged?
TOM:	I am not deranged, Miss Polly.
POLLY:	Papa?
FRANKLIN:	The prisoner is of sound mind, but do keep him covered while I bandage the wound.
TOM:	I am wounded by your daughter and my sister?

Franklin slaps Tom, then continues to bandage his wound.

FRANKLIN:	I'll have a doctor dress the wound the first thing tomorrow morning. When he asks what caused the wound, you are to say a bullet fired by someone in the mob struck you.
TOM:	I am to lie to the physician?
FRANKLIN:	It will do no good to have it known that you were shot while attempting to escape.
POLLY:	The fire in Hoyden's eyes was that of a mad man filled with revenge and rage. I must know what course of action awaits us.
TOM:	They will sound the tower bell in the town square at midnight. And then I shall be no more.

FRANKLIN: If they come, you must say nothing to give Hoyden the power he so hungrily wants.

Polly can't take her eyes away from Tom.

POLLY: Now that I am able to see and hear the prisoner more clearly, I can't help but notice his likeness to you. Even his speech is that of an educated man.

FRANKLIN: Now is not the time to talk about it.

POLLY: Papa, please! I watched you at breakfast.

FRANKLIN: What did you notice?

POLLY: The strange manner in which you were acting.

FRANKLIN: Of course, Polly. I was exhausted from the long search.

POLLY: Is that why you poured salt into your coffee and vinegar over your pancakes? You didn't take notice until you tasted them.

FRANKLIN: Captain Walker's death has shaken us all.

POLLY: My dear father, you have never been one to shrink from the truth. I don't expect you to do so now.

Franklin treads cautiously, measuring his words.

FRANKLIN: If I could push aside the flesh and all its passions and prejudices long enough for the acts of my life to stand out in the clear light of truth, you would see your father as God himself sees him.

POLLY: Please speak directly to the subject. Am I not your only child?

FRANKLIN: Many Southern white men knew their household servants in such a manner as I knew the prisoner's mother.

POLLY: Cicely, you mean?

FRANKLIN: Yes.

TOM: Your father knew my mother intimately.

POLLY: Papa? You must tell me it isn't so.

FRANKLIN: As you say, I have never been one to shrink from the truth.

POLLY: Then it is so?

FRANKLIN:	I can't in the eyes of God shake off the consequences of my sin.

After a moment, Polly speaks.

POLLY:	Had you never sinned, this wayward spirit would not have come back from the vanished past to haunt us.
FRANKLIN:	I should have sent Tom and Cicely north to Canada or to England and France to turn their life pursuits into something more humanly productive.
TOM:	You could have kept us on the plantation.
FRANKLIN:	That would not have been possible.
POLLY:	How much is known of this in Branson County?
FRANKLIN:	The truth be known, not a person I know is without sin.
POLLY:	Papa, please!
FRANKLIN:	You saw that in the lynch mob. Even our most respectable citizens of this county—doctors, lawyers, and preachers—would have murdered an innocent prisoner without forethought.
POLLY:	How can you say innocent when you don't know? He is certain to hang.
FRANKLIN:	The prisoner will not die by a crazed lynch mob. I stand on my word.
POLLY:	One man against the world. You are a mad man!
FRANKLIN:	If Deputy Hoyden is the measure of sanity in Branson County, the world is turned upside down.

Molly is suddenly shaken by something outside that Franklin doesn't yet hear.

POLLY:	Papa, I hear quiet footsteps.
FRANKLIN:	Don't let your imagination get the best of you.
TOM:	She's not imagining. The earth shudders beneath the rage of the mob.
POLLY:	What must we do?
TOM:	Yes, what must we do, Sheriff.
POLLY:	The prisoner has no claim to our lives.

FRANKLIN:	Must I repeat myself?
POLLY:	Only a mad man would try and stop the mob.

Shadows move by. Muted voices are heard outside. Polly draws close to her father.

FRANKLIN:	Are they the men God would have leading Branson County back to civilization? I think not.
TOM:	Release me to the mob and get it over with now.
FRANKLIN:	You are my prisoner and my duty.
TOM:	Am I not your son?
POLLY:	Papa?
TOM:	The bastard child you sired by your slave Cicely?

Hearing noise, Franklin responds to Tom in a whispered shout.

FRANKLIN:	Quiet!

There is a suspenseful silence. Several shots ring out. Franklin fires back several times.

FRANKLIN:	I'm warning you. Get control of your mob, Hoyden.

Hoyden speaks from outside.

HOYDEN:	Hold your fire! Quiet, everybody!

Hoyden enters. He is feeling his oats.

FRANKLIN:	I'm listening.
HOYDEN:	We the members of the Branson County Organizing Committee believe you got further investment in the captain's murder.
FRANKLIN:	You deserved to be shot on the spot for uttering such a thought. Order your men to depart.
HOYDEN:	Ain't no turning back. The prisoner is going to pay for his crime.
FRANKLIN:	Judge Washington has to convene a grand jury.

HOYDEN:	The Honorable Judge Washington just died of a heart attack. God rest his soul. Seems that he knowd more about your family history than his poor heart could bear. His dying wish is that you be removed from the case without further delay.
FRANKLIN:	Explain yourself, Hoyden.
HOYDEN:	Nothing to explain. You're blind as a bat if you can't see your reflection in the prisoner. You're done for as Branson County Sheriff. Legal authority to carry out the wishes of the citizens is now in my hands.
FRANKLIN:	You're God himself now. Is that it?
HOYDEN:	Being that you're locked inside the jail with your entire family, you could say that. Ain't much a man can do to uphold the law from behind bars.
FRANKLIN:	Hoyden, you're in no shape to uphold the law. You reek of Carson's moonshine.
HOYDEN:	You've got two choices. Release the prisoner to us, or let us inside to take him.
POLLY:	And if Papa chooses not to hand over the prisoner?
HOYDEN:	We're taking him by force.
POLLY:	Papa, what must we do?
HOYDEN:	I'd sure hate to see something happen to Miss Polly.
FRANKLIN:	I'll tell you what I'm going to do . . .
HOYDEN:	Franklin—*I'm* telling *you* what *you're* going to do.
FRANKLIN:	Don't force my hand, Hoyden.
HOYDEN:	That's Deputy Hoyden to you. Now, you're going to release Miss Polly to the organizing committee.
POLLY:	I will not be separated from my father.
HOYDEN:	Is that the way you want it?
FRANKLIN:	Polly, go on outside.
POLLY:	I'm not going anyplace without you by my side.
FRANLIN:	You will obey your father.
POLLY:	Papa . . .
FRANKLIN:	Go quickly.

Polly embraces her father.

POLLY:	I'll never see you again!
HOYDEN:	Now, that being done, you will release the prisoner to me.
FRANKLIN:	Nothing further happens until Polly is safely delivered to the women on the edge of the crowd.
HOYDEN:	So be it. Doc Caine!
FRANKLIN:	Stop! Doc isn't to set one foot in the direction of this jail.
HOYDEN:	Stay put, Doc!
FRANKLIN:	You will report back to me when Polly is safely delivered. That's an order, Hoyden.
HOYDEN:	As you say.
FRANKLIN:	If anyone in your group lays a finger of harm on Polly, I am taking on the mob singlehandedly.
HOYDEN:	I'm taking her over now.
FRANKLIN:	Don't move another step.

Hoyden stops.

HOYDEN:	I stopped, but that don't mean I'm conceding.
FRANKLIN:	What do you propose to do to the prisoner?

Hoyden speaks with a quiet rage etched in triumph.

HOYDEN:	The midnight picnic is still on. You're invited.

Franklin stares at Hoyden, as if looking straight through him.

POLLY:	Must you delay the inevitable?
FRANKLIN:	Lynching an innocent man is not inevitable.
HOYDEN:	Listen to your daughter, Franklin.
FRANKLIN:	That's Sheriff Franklin.
HOYDEN:	Not anymore.
FRANKLIN:	Good-bye, Polly.
POLLY:	Papa!
FRANKLIN:	Polly . . .

With much difficulty, Franklin looks away to avoid seeing Polly go.

| POLLY: | Noooo! You mustn't leave me. |

Hoyden exits, holding up a weakened Polly.

TOM:	Too bad your daughter didn't kill me. She would have spared us this most horrific spectacle.
FRANKLIN:	My daughter is a straight shooter. It's the reason you're alive. Did you murder Captain Walker?
TOM:	I am not a murderer.
FRANKLIN:	You would be if Polly hadn't come to my rescue.
TOM:	You wouldn't have died by my hands.
FRANKLIN:	You dare to dispute me?
TOM:	The hand of my mother—and your former slave, Cicely—held the trigger that spared your life. She would never have allowed me to kill the man who gave me life.
FRANKLIN:	Why did you come back here?
TOM:	I promised my mother I would do everything within my power to find her relatives, except I knew no one. So I gave up and tried to let go, but her tortured face chased me night and day until the only thing left for me in the world was to take to the road without money or food.
FRANKLIN:	Your mother has no surviving relatives here.
TOM:	As much as it pains me to say so, you are the only kin I have left in the world that I know of. Except for the ancestral blood coursing through our veins, we have no God-given reason to call each other family.
FRANKLIN:	That's not what brought you to the captain's home.
TOM:	No it wasn't. I saw this old man, and I followed him at a distance for several days praying to God that he was someone who needed help for hire. I hoped to get work around his house to secure food and clothing. Then, one day, with my mother's voice urging me on, I found the courage to knock at his door. He didn't come down. I presumed the old man to be napping. And so I came back the next

	day. No answer. When he didn't come down on the third day, I entered the house.
FRANKLIN:	And you took food.
TOM:	What is a starving man to do? I started grabbing food and clothes to sustain myself for a couple of days. That's when I heard someone suddenly moving around upstairs. I grabbed the old man's coat and fled into the dark.
FRANKLIN:	You never got a glimpse of the prowler?
TOM:	If only I had lingered nearby to see him.
FRANKLIN:	You couldn't make out the sound of his voice?
TOM:	God forbid, I was too frightened to take notice. Had I stopped to investigate, I fear I'd have been shot and killed.
FRANKLIN:	You must have an alibi if your life is to be spared.
TOM:	I've told you the truth. What more can I offer?
FRANKLIN:	Is there a white man in Branson County who can vouch for your presence elsewhere at the time of Captain Walker's murder?
TOM:	My dear mother Cicely and God are my only witnesses.
FRANKLIN:	They don't count in Branson County.
TOM:	You are the only one I know in Branson County.
FRANKLIN:	I know you as Captain Walker's murderer.
TOM:	If God matters not to the lynch mob, and you know me not, my life on this earth is soon to be no more.
FRANKLIN:	The city passed an ordinance after the last lynching that all prisoners in Branson County are guaranteed a fair trial.
TOM:	No earthly law stands a chance against a crazed mob.
FRANKLIN:	I am bound by duty to protect you.

The bell sounds. Noise of the mob rises. Tom stares at Franklin, then speaks with cautious resolve.

TOM:	There, now. The bell tolls for me. I must know the answer to one question for my mother's sake. Did you love Cicely?

Franklin hesitates. Then he speaks in measured tone.

FRANKLIN: I loved Cicely to the extent that a master was permitted to love his slave.

TOM: Your *love* for her did not extend deep enough to keep my mother off the auction block. Circumstance compelled you to sell her to the highest bidder.

FRANKLIN: For that, I must answer to God.

TOM: You are compelled by circumstance once again—this time to release Cicely's only living child to a lynch mob.

After a contemplative moment, Franklin speaks with a quiet resolve.

FRANKLIN: I give you my word. They will not take you.

TOM: Sheriff, I am no fool. I know what happened to the last Negro lynched in Branson County. He greeted a white woman and failed to cross to the other side of the street.

Franklin is taken aback by Tom's surprising statement, but tries to remain calm.

FRANKLIN: How did you find out about the lynching? You were far away.

TOM: The terrifying news struck like a dagger in the heart of every Negro household in America. How could they have done such a godforsaken deed? The lynch victim himself was the slave master's son. He was lynched for committing the crime of greeting his own sister. God forbid. I have committed the crime of entering Branson County in search of my mother's kin.

Hoyden enters.

HOYDEN:	You got sixty seconds to hand over the prisoner.
FRANKLIN:	The prisoner is guaranteed a fair trial. It's the law.
HOYDEN:	Captain Walker's murderer has no choice in this matter. The same goes for you Franklin. He is now the property of the Branson County Organizing Committee.
FRANKLIN:	I'm warning you, Hoyden.
TOM:	No need to hand me over. I shall walk out on my own accord.

Tom moves slowly toward the door.

FRANKLIN:	Halt!
TOM:	Why must I?
FRANKLIN:	Please . . .
TOM:	My lynching started the day I was born a Negro.

Tom opens door. He steps slowly into doorway, slowly putting one foot outside. Franklin shouts out to Tom in utter desperation.

FRANKLIN:	I beg of you!

Tom turns and stares at Sheriff Franklin, a longing of hope in his eyes.

TOM:	You can't stop the picnic.

Tom turns and takes a stop towards the door, then he raises his hands in surrender.

FRANKLIN:	Tom!

Franklin shoots. Tom falls backwards as Franklin rushes forward and catches him in his arms. He lifts Tom's body off the floor in his arms. Hoyden stares dumbfounded. Franklin looks at Hoyden and speaks with authority and resolve.

FRANKLIN:	The midnight picnic is cancelled by order of the Branson County Sheriff.

Hoyden looks on in silent defeat. He makes his way to the door with no words upon his lips.

Lights down.

End of Play

CLASS AND COLOR WITHIN BLACK AMERICA

The year was 1948. *Ebony*, America's preeminent black magazine, called the history-making event a triumph for wronged Negro motherhood. No, it wasn't on a scale comparable to U.S. President Harry Truman signing the executive order that ended racial segregation in the United States Armed Forces, or the Marshall Plan authorizing $5 billion to rebuild Europe following World War II. Nor did it compare to the excitement of the Cleveland Indians defeating the Boston Braves four games to two in the Baseball World Series—all of which took place in 1948. The history-making event to which *Ebony* referred was, however, an intracultural milestone for Black America. A dark-skinned beauty was crowned "Miss Fine Brown Frame" in a Harlem beauty contest. The way it happened was even more remarkable. The judges were about to award the crown to a fair-skinned—but racially "black"—"Dixie Belle"; but the angry audience rebelled, forcing them to offer a compromise: the cash award for the dark beauty and the title for the fair-skinned African American beauty. The riled up audience was unyielding in their demand that justice not be denied the dark-skinned beauty. The judges relented, and Evelyn Sanders was crowned "Miss Fine Brown Frame." Miss Sanders's cash award and promised movie contract were not so readily forthcoming. Yet she had made history. Indeed, no young lady darker than olive had ever been seriously considered for the Cotton Club chorus line before 1932.

This is one reflection of the world of intraracial discrimination rarely acknowledged in American society at large, although it is well-known if mostly whispered about in African American society. My purpose here is to briefly explore this racial phenomenon and its social consequences as they have historically impacted interracial and intraracial relationships in the United States. Hopefully, it will help to blunt the social stigma attached to dark skin that continues to plague American society, particularly those African Americans who have borne the brunt of this degradation. Only then can white and black Americans better understand the complex nature of skin color dynamics within our society as a basis for developing a greater appreciation of dark skin as inclusive of the cultural norm characteristic of a racially diverse society.

Consider the following evidence: African Americans, many of whom came of age during the fifties and sixties, remember all too well the bleach-and-glow advertisements that promised fairer skin and the "process" or "conked" hairdos of black male entertainers who despaired over their kinky African locks in their efforts to create a crossover appeal to white audiences. It was a time when many fair-skinned blacks negotiated challenging racial barriers by crossing the color line and assimilating into white America. Consenting black relatives and friends winked, nodded their approval, and looked the other way. In what may be perhaps the most extreme case to date, and what might be construed as a form of "whitewashing," National Association for the Advancement of Colored People (NAACP) President, Walter White, himself a blond black man, aroused the wrath of many African Americans when he authored an article about a newly developed chemical that could possibly wipe out the color line because it purportedly could change Blacks to white. Even though some black and white Americans thought this chemical leap would instantly overcome hundreds of years of racial barriers in between, missing from the equation was a comparable solution that would transform other physical characteristics commonly identified with people born of African ancestry into socially acceptable European features.

It is important to note here that interracial relationships among Europeans and Africans, the primary basis for "colorism" in our society, have existed in what is now the United States of America since the earliest colonies. Anti-miscegenation laws enacted to prohibit such relationships date as far back as 1664 in Maryland and 1691 in Virginia. And they remained in effect until Loving v. Virginia in 1967 when the United States Supreme Court unanimously ruled that anti-miscegenation laws were unconstitutional. Despite being in effect since the latter half of the seventeenth century, it was sometime later before anti-miscegenation laws became commonplace in most states. While the earliest of such laws appear to be motivated largely by the economics of slavery, later laws were aimed primarily at keeping black men from white women. It was no secret that many African Americans were the offspring of white Americans, including some very prominent whites—with Thomas Jefferson being the most famous. But unlike the era of apartheid in South Africa and the emergence of class and color in some Latin American countries, America never enacted national laws that distinguished between light and dark-skinned Americans of African descent. All, regardless of their hue, were subjected to the same Jim Crow laws. Even those who bore a glaring resemblance to their European relatives were "tainted" with the blood of Africa, and one drop of African blood was the standard that determined their status as "Negro." Charles Chesnutt, author of the short stories on which the two plays in this book are based, could have easily passed for white.

The absence of national laws favoring Blacks of European ancestry did not prevent the emergence of a color caste within black society. Many Blacks took great pride in their prominent European features. Understandably so, especially given that such features were often viewed as a status symbol within the African American community. A few even reaped the benefits of inheritances from their white parents, while others were among the first to attend newly established black colleges following the Civil War and, subsequently, the postbellum era. The overwhelming number of Blacks elected to office during Reconstruction, for example, was of mixed race—a trend that continued through the civil rights era—and it is a circumstance still reflected in the U.S. Congress and state governments to this day.

Ironically, the color caste system that arose out of a society that embraced its European ancestry was not recognized by European Americans. As is often the case, Blacks who subscribed to such class distinctions associated primarily with members from within their own social circles, thus creating what amounted to an informal apartheid. This "informal" apartheid was not without its complications, as it was influenced by certain geographical, political, and socioeconomic factors. Given the limited choices available to them, it could mean spinsterhood for women who did not find a suitable mate of a similar color; while in other cases, it meant marrying someone of a lesser status but who met the color standard. In the case of fair-skinned women, a dark-skinned husband who had achieved a respectable level of status and power was an acceptable mate, especially since it carried mutual benefits for both spouses. Many light-skinned and dark-skinned black families never made color an issue, while some openly discriminated along color lines within the same household, unwittingly teaching their children discrimination since, of course, the family is a child's first and primary source of education about race and color.

It is worth noting here that outliers of all groups, mostly out of necessity and sometimes outright defiance, have historically flaunted anti-miscegenation laws while the community quietly looked the other way. The concept of race, after all, is influenced by expediency, political, legal, and otherwise, thus calling into question the notion of race as a fixed identity. Racial identity is further influenced by those with authority and power to determine another's racial status, even if capriciously so, for the sake of conformity and also as a requisite for documentation. For instance, one interracially married black female recently noted how color had influenced the local school board's identification of her three children, with one listed as black, the second as Latino, and the third as white.

The civil rights era of the sixties and early seventies brought with it a strong sense of pride in African American society and culture in which identity was heavily influenced by skin color. Afros, the popular hairstyles of the sixties and seventies, dashikis, and other prominent cultural artifacts challenged the prevailing cultural norm that associated dark skin with social deviation. Even corporate America joined in the movement, not just because it was morally appropriate, but because it also became financially profitable to do so. Some personnel managers did not hesitate to make sure that African Americans in the most conspicuous positions were unmistakably black, while those of a lighter hue sometimes found themselves victims of reverse discrimination, even targets of contempt from their darker brothers and sisters.

During the 1990s, color and caste within black society became the subject of major talk shows, such as *Oprah* and *Phil Donahue*. The issue was also addressed on the now defunct but critically acclaimed television series *Frank's Place*. It has been written about in *Essence* and *Ebony* magazines. Even the *New York Times* ran a front page article on the subject. Among Blacks, for example, it is common knowledge that the caste system reflected in the *Blue Vein Society* extended to historically black colleges where it included organizations whose members were comprised mostly of fair-complexioned students such as cheerleaders and kick-line dance teams, as well as certain sororities and fraternities. That we can talk openly about the issue is testimony to how far we have come in being comfortable with addressing a subject that was once confined to the "colored" closet.

But make no mistake about it, intraracial class and color discrimination has by no means disappeared. Nor is the problem sufficiently camouflaged beneath the pretense of a color-blind society. The documentary *Dark Girls,* directed by Bill Duke and D. Channsin Berry, presents a disturbing portrait of dark-skinned women as victims of intraracial and interracial discrimination and the searing emotional scars that come with their painful experiences. The most devastating comments to these women's self-esteem, often innocently noted in casual remarks, are likely to come from their closest relative, the mother, potentially triggering a lifelong identity crisis. The CNN series "Black in America," hosted by CNN anchorwoman Soledad O'Brien, recently presented an installment called "Who Is Black in America?" One major theme from the segment reveals that the extent to which participants valued and respected their black identity was clearly influenced by the attitudes of parents and family.

Intracultural racism can quickly rear its ugly head in interactions with immigrants from countries where the preference for fair skin still remains the unspoken rule. A colleague at the City University of New York (CUNY) noted that a dark-skinned Jamaican student defined himself as fair-skinned on an assignment that asked students how they would identify their skin color. My colleague questioned the young man on the interpretation of his response, whereupon he pointed out that in his native Jamaica, status and power were associated with his fellow lighter-skinned countrymen who held the best jobs and most favorable government positions. Without hesitation, he observed that he planned to marry a white woman as a means of improving his status and that of his future children. While this may appear shocking to some of us, a quick Internet search reveals a plethora of ads promoting cosmetics that guarantee a fairer complexion, thereby connecting lighter skin to a more socially acceptable appearance and therefore professional advancement.

Skin color isn't just about race and racism; it has become a huge business, particularly at the international level. Asian and African women are the major targets of such ads, especially those residing in countries where color is often reflected in the caste system and where women are the most likely to be victimized. No wonder then that international beauty queens from certain Asian countries are known to take pills to lighten their complexion in order to conform more closely to the homogenized European look that was once so popular in the Miss World and Miss Universe beauty pageants. In the case of Africa, the World Health Organization (WHO) released a report in June 2012 stating that 77% of Nigerian women use some form of skin-bleaching products. The percentage in Togo, Senegal, Mali, and South Africa is also substantial. For many women, especially those who spend a disproportionate amount of their meager income on such products, the high cost of keeping up the fair skin appearance is more likely to promote poverty and poor health rather than socioeconomic advancement. From a business point of view, however, skin bleaching is good news. Sales are in the billions of dollars for corporations producing and marketing these products.

Despite lagging acceptance of diversity based on skin color, intraracially and interracially, at the international level, the United States has made substantial progress in these areas. Even so, most would agree that we still have work to do. However, addressing black intraracial discrimination remains complicated to this very day because, historically, anti-miscegenation laws and the "one drop" rule sent the unambiguous message that the fate of light and dark-skinned Blacks was irrevocably linked. This, in turn, necessitated the appearance of an unshakeable allegiance within black culture that remained intact until laws promoting racial equality were firmly entrenched in the early seventies more than a hundred years after the Emancipation Proclamation. Such a long and indivisible unified front virtually rendered moot notions of intraracial discrimination as a cause deserving anything more than cursory attention.

Thus it remains difficult to address intraracial class and color differences on almost any legal or policy level, even though we know that dark-skinned African Americans are most likely to be ensnared within the criminal justice system; are likely to be judged more harshly by black and white jurors than white and fair-skinned blacks; and they are the group most likely to be found at the bottom of the socioeconomic ladder. Besides, given the complicated relationships within black culture, even within and among individual and extended families, most African Americans would balk at airing their so-called "dirty laundry" in any legal venue, class and color notwithstanding. Intraracial discrimination remains practically invisible to white America and the federal government views it as more of an intracultural matter than an affirmative action issue. Further complicating the situation is the new reality that opportunities to assimilate racially and economically have created more diverse and complex racial identities in which many highly successful Blacks, light and dark-skinned, no longer feel any allegiance to "elevating" the race—this despite the fact that most are the beneficiaries of the efforts of those dedicated black leaders who led the struggle to pave the way for their success.

In exploring intraracial issues in the context of fiction, Charles Waddell Chesnutt is very much a visionary and a muckraker who takes on the taboo subject of white and black racism in the late nineteenth and early twentieth century. In his short story, "A Matter of Principle," Chesnutt reveals the heart and mind of the lead character, Cicero Clayton, a fair-skinned man who refuses to accept the prevailing racial mentality that members of the Blue Vein Society should be subjected to the same "social ostracism" as darker African Americans. "But I don't accept this classification, for my part, and I imagine that, as the chief party in interest, I have a right to my opinion. People who belong by half or more of their blood to the most virile and progressive race of modern times has as much right to call themselves white as others have to call them negroes." It's fair to say that Clayton saw himself as superior to not just dark-skinned Black Americans but to poor whites, yet he occupied a status below poor whites on the totem pole of color because his African ancestry differentiated him from them, thereby denying him the equal access and power that came with "pure" European ancestry.

A victim of internalized racism himself, Clayton treats Blacks according to the intensity of their skin color, meaning those with the most prominent African features rank at the bottom of the ladder of social acceptability. There are exceptions, one being a handful of Blacks who have achieved a level of respectability and social standing beyond which skin color matters very little. After all, power and money usually do trump color in any society. Similarly, in "The Wife of His Youth," one of Chesnutt's most popular short stories, on which *The Blue Vein Society* is based, Mr. Ryder's ascendency to the head of the Blue Vein Society provides a cover for him to conceal his past as a fugitive slave, thus no one suspects that he is anything other than a Blue Vein Society blueblood. Ryder's new status has resulted in an identity change that now works to his advantage. As gatekeeper of the Blue Vein Society, Ryder uses his authority and power to bend the rules to promote his interests, which includes accepting men of prominence even when they fail to meet the color requirements. Yet he rigidly enforces the rules at his convenience. So when he chooses to enforce a rule that excludes former slaves aimed at keeping out dark-skinned Blacks, he is unaware that he is excluding the very beautiful and educated woman he has come to love. However, it is the sudden appearance of his wife from slavery that creates an unforeseen dilemma that threatens to destroy Ryder's social standing within the community. He is, in a word, forced to confront his hidden identity.

There is a redeeming quality in Chesnutt's view of the Blue Vein Society that appears to mirror his own life. Society members represent a burgeoning wave of middle-class Black Americans who have climbed the social ladder of success through hard work, therefore mirroring the familiar sweat-and-toil work-ethic characteristic of America in general during this era. To his credit, Ryder has worked his way up the ladder of success to become the most prominent black man in Groveland, an achievement even the most diehard racist is compelled to respect. In Chesnutt's own life, as well as in much of his fiction, successful Blacks shared a commitment to "elevating" the race even if they were not unanimous in their agreement on how it should happen. Their lifelong efforts can be seen through memberships in those organizations that promoted social justice and racial equality, the most prominent being the NAACP, which remains very active in the fight for justice and equality. Indeed, this unfailing group allegiance, often seen operating today in political elections and commitment to social causes, may appear paradoxical, but it remains a reality that continues to characterize the complex race relations within Black America and within America in general.

Finally, in contrast to the "scientific racism" of the late nineteenth and early twentieth century that prevailed during Chesnutt's day, and which was used to justify European Imperialism, the twenty-first century focus on diversity has come to support some anthropological claims that advance the theory that we are all descendants of one mother from Africa. If that is the case, we have a great deal to be proud of and much for which we should be ashamed. For as the great African-American educator and leader

Mary McLeod Bethune tells us in her *Last Will and Testament*: "Our aim must be to create a world of fellowship and justice where no person's skin color or religion is held against him." To this end, Chesnutt and Bethune, two people of color, one who cherished the purity of her African roots and the other who took great pride in his European ancestry, shared a common goal: justice and equality for all.

CHARLES WADDELL CHESNUTT

Charles Waddell Chesnutt was born June 20, 1858, in Cleveland, Ohio. Parents Andrew Jackson Chesnutt and Ann Maria (Sampson) had met the previous year while moving with a group of free persons of color from Fayetteville, North Carolina, to Cleveland. Chesnutt returned to Fayetteville with his family in 1867. He attended the Howard School, a Freedman's Bureau school that his father helped to establish. He began teaching at age thirteen while still a student at the Howard school. He later taught in Charlotte, North Carolina, and in South Carolina before returning home to become assistant principal at the Fayetteville School, which had by then been reestablished as the State Colored Normal School, a land grant institution to train teachers. Chesnutt married Susan Perry, a school teacher, and in 1880 was promoted to school principal.

Precocious, industrious, and ambitious, Chesnutt engaged in private studies that included Latin, German, French, and algebra. And he kept abreast of the works of the prominent literary figures of his day. He also trained as a stenographer and was an organist and choirmaster at his Fayetteville church. Chesnutt was acutely attuned to the black and white worlds in which he lived and interacted. Paradoxically, as a mixed race person who could pass for white, Chesnutt felt alienated from both. The good life and notoriety for which he yearned was not to be had in the destitute black community where he lived and worked. Despite the fact that he projected a keen sensibility for European culture and lifestyle, his "one drop" of African blood prevented him from being accepted into the white world. The impatient and ambitious Chesnutt was not willing to accept the status quo. Rather, he was compelled to fight for justice with the most potent weapon at his disposal, the *written word*, choosing fiction as the primary vehicle of choice to convey his message.

As a young man coming of age during the 1870s, Chesnutt saw the evisceration of the Reconstruction Amendments through the rise of Jim Crow laws and Supreme Court decisions backing racial segregation that reestablished white supremacy and effectively consigned African Americans to second-class citizens. Chesnutt was a member of the growing black middle class, a group in which fair skin carried prestige and power among the more educated free persons of color and their descendents. This world experience would provide the fodder for much of Chesnutt's fiction as evidenced in such highly sensitive issues as interracial and intraracial class and color discrimination, miscegenation, the evolving African American family, and black economic self-sufficiency.

Chesnutt had the foremost exemplary literary figures of his day as role models, two of whom were Ohio natives, including William Dean Howells, famous novelist and *Atlantic Monthly* editor, who would become known as the "Dean of American Letters." And there was the radical Reconstruction lawyer, judge, and novelist Albion W. Tourgee. The latter, also a Civil War veteran of the Union Army, settled in Greensborough, North Carolina, where he became famous for his best-selling Reconstruction era novel, *A Fool's Errand, by One of the Fools* (1879). A third and highly famous Midwesterner was master novelist Mark Twain, known for his most famous works, the *Adventures of Tom Sawyer* (1876) and *The Adventures of Huckleberry Finn* (1885). And most important in the area of social reform was the African American abolitionist and former slave Fredrick Douglass, living proof of the intellectual, oratorical, and literary heights to which a former slave could rise if given the opportunity. What better evidence could be found than in Douglass's *Narrative of the Life of Fredrick Douglass, an American Slave* (1845) and *Life and Times of Fredrick Douglass* (1881). Chesnutt's readership would be mostly white, but unlike his white contemporaries, his challenge would be complicated by his identity as a white black man on a mission for social and racial justice. Chesnutt resigned his position as school principal at the State Colored Normal School and moved to New York in1883. But after a brief period as a reporter for Dow, Jones and Company in New York City, he settled in Cleveland where he passed the bar, started a highly successful legal stenography business, and pursued his literary interests.

Chesnutt's literary breakthrough came with the publication of his critically acclaimed short story, "The Goophered Grapevine," which appeared in the *Atlantic Monthly* in August 1887, thus making Chesnutt the first African American to be published in the prestigious magazine. His first two books were short story collections published in 1899 by Houghton Mifflin and Company. The first book, a collection of seven short stories entitled *The Conjure Woman*, introduces the Uncle Julius character, a freed slave who is highly adept at spinning humorous but self-serving versions of life in the South for the entertainment of his white audience. Cast in the mold of the Uncle Remus stories published by journalist Joel Chandler Harris and Thomas Nelson Page some years earlier, some criticized Chesnutt for depicting offensive black stereotypes. But a closer reading of Chesnutt's stories finds Uncle Julius more subtle, complex, and sophisticated in explaining his relationship to the postbellum South in which he must negotiate and maneuver for the sake of his own economic survival. In Chesnutt's world, Uncle Julius does not merely entertain whites, but he wears the mask as the trickster on a mission, in much the same way that Chesnutt is on a mission, though not as obviously so as he proves to be in his subsequent stories.

The Wife of His Youth and Other Stories of the Color Line, Chesnutt's second book, was also published by Houghton Mifflin and Company in 1899. It is much more direct in addressing intraracial and interracial issues such as miscegenation, class and, color as they impacted blacks who were fair enough to pass for white, reflecting Chesnutt's own experiences and relationships. With the publication of *The Wife of His Youth and Other Stories of the Color Line,* Chesnutt's status as a successful writer was cemented. Howells praised Chesnutt in the *Atlantic Monthly* in an article that reviewed the two books. In addition to his collection of short stories that were published in 1899, Chesnutt also published *Fredrick Douglass*, the biography of the African American abolitionist Frederick Douglass. Chesnutt's success as a writer during this time led him to close his stenography business and devote full time to writing.

The House Behind the Cedars, Chesnutt's first novel, published in 1900 by Houghton Mifflin and Company, follows more closely in the tradition of *The Wife of His Youth and Other Stories of the Color Line* with its focus on miscegenation and passing. In the novel, mulatto brother and sister, John and Lena Walden, are fair enough to pass for white and do so as a matter of convenience, as a way of gaining economic advantage, and even out of romantic interest when Lena finds herself the object of affection by a white suitor. They are forced to navigate a treacherous road as they move back and forth between separate black and white worlds, not so much because of the color of their skin, but perceptions of race and the "one drop" rule demand it. Chesnutt shows the high cost, even tragic consequences, of racism at a time when the evolving black middle class is constrained by regressive racial laws. This did not make for comfortable subject matter for Chesnutt's mostly white readers, many of whom who were more at ease with the Uncle Julius stories in the *Conjure Woman* than they were with interracial and intraracial relationships.

But as a writer on a mission, Chesnutt was compelled to write even more painful stories, especially in the face of increasing violence and terrorism against African Americans. The *Marrow of Tradition,* Chesnutt's second novel, published in 1901 by Houghton Mifflin and Company, was based on the Wilmington, North Carolina, Massacre of 1898, also referred to as the Wilmington Race Riot. Members of Chesnutt's own family were witnesses to the events, which no doubt deeply influenced his approach to writing about a story in which angry whites had thrown out the elected biracial government and established their own in one of the most violent and brazen displays of white supremacy in American history. Chesnutt's novel provided a counterpoint to the prevailing versions of the massacre that were depicted in southern white newspapers and fiction around the same time. He was sophisticated enough to know that many stories about such incidents were often written to persuade the northern press and reader to accept the default version by the white media, leaving black voices mute to white America, except for the black press. Not shying away from the incendiary political issues, Chesnutt reveals his own passionate aversion to racial bigotry and violence directed at African Americans. The *Marrow of Tradition* was a bitter pill to swallow, even for Chesnutt's ardent supporters, including William Dean Howells. The resulting poor sales of *Marrow of Tradition* forced Chesnutt to resume his stenography business.

Houghton Mifflin and Company rejected Chesnutt's third and final novel to be published during his lifetime, *The Colonel's Dream*. It was published by Doubleday in 1905. In *The Colonel's Dream*, Chesnutt appears to be calling for the unthinkable for the novel's time, a kind of southern utopia of racial, social, and economic equality with blacks and whites living together in a harmonious world. Indeed, Chesnutt appears to be three quarters of a century ahead of his time, dooming his career as a writer.

Set in Clarendon, North Carolina, just a few years after the Wilmington Massacre of 1898. Colonel Henry French, a Clarendon native and Civil War veteran, sells his successful business venture in New York and returns home with his young son, initially on advice of his doctor for health reasons, but memories of his hometown compel him to remain, except he is now a new man committed to turning his hometown into a model community where social and racial equality becomes the norm. Colonel French meets furious resistance at every turn as he encounters classism, racism, corruption, exploitation of black workers through low wages, long work hours, and poor working conditions—even miscegenation. The close-minded citizens of Clarendon, with the backing of the newspaper editor, are determined to keep the Blacks in their place. In the end, racial violence and hatred are worse than they were before the colonel arrived. He gives up and returns to his previous business in New York City.

In some ways, the Colonel's giving up mirrored Chesnutt's literary career, as this would be the last novel published during his lifetime. The novel sold poorly and his readers abandoned him. Chesnutt, as a literary figure, would languish in obscurity for many years, even overshadowed by the Harlem Renaissance literary writers, such as James Weldon Johnson, Langston Hughes, Claude McKay, Countee Cullen, and others. Renewed interest in his work during the sixties and seventies would eventually restore Chesnutt to his place as one of the country's most important African American literary figures. Chesnutt did not disappear from the public, not by any means. As a businessman, he focused primarily on his lucrative legal stenography business. He also stayed active in civil rights for the remainder of his life. The National Association for the Advancement of Colored People (NACCP) awarded him the Spingarn Medal in 1928. He died on November 15, 1932.

There has been a substantial amount of critical scholarship on Chesnutt and his writings since the 1990s. His unpublished novels, short fiction, and essays have since been published, and many of his works are now available online. For the beginning Chesnutt reader, I do recommend several publications as a starting point. The most recent is the Norton Anthology publication of *Marrow of Tradition,* published in May 2012. It is the 1901 edition, with an introduction and notes on the text by Werner Sollors. Additional materials that include writings related to the event have been published in this edition. Also recommended is the Library of America publication, *Charles W. Chesnutt: Stories, Novels, and Essays* (2002). It includes *The Conjure Woman, The Wife of His Youth and Other Stories of the Color Line, The House Behind the Cedars, The Marrow of Tradition*, and numerous essays that reflect Chesnutt's vision on race and class in America. It is also edited by Werner Sollors with additional notes on the texts and a highly useful chronology on Chesnutt's life.

Several other books deserve to be noted here. *The Northern Stories by Charles W. Chesnutt*, edited by Charles Duncan, provides commentary and analysis of short fiction and essays written by Chesnutt that are mostly set in the North. There is *The Portable Charles W. Chesnutt,* edited by William Andrews, with Henry Louis Gates Jr. as the general editor. Gates also wrote the introduction. It is an excellent starting point for those seeking a more scholarly interpretation of Chesnutt's work in the Penguin edition. Finally, for those seeking a more recent critical perspective on Chesnutt, there is Ryan Simmons's study, *Chesnutt and Realism: A Study of the Novels.* Simmons situates Chesnutt in a new light in the realist tradition that sets him apart from his white contemporaries, especially William Dean Howells and Mark Twain, in that he is influenced by his ethnic and world experience as an African American.

No one in Chesnutt's time could have imagined that more than a century after his last novel much of what he wrote about would come to pass.

> To the great number of those who are seeking, in whatever manner or degree, from near at hand or far away, to bring the forces of enlightenment to bear upon the vexed problems which harass the South, this volume is inscribed, with the hope that it may contribute to the same good end.
>
> If there be nothing new between its covers, neither is love new, nor faith, nor hope, nor disappointment, nor sorrow. Yet life is not the less worth living because of any of these, nor has any man truly lived until he has tasted of them all.
>
> —Charles W. Chesnutt
> "Dedication" to the novel *The Colonel's Dream*

ABOUT THE PLAYWRIGHT

Sam Kelley first came to the attention of the theatre community with the production of his critically acclaimed play *Pill Hill*, which premiered at the Yale Repertory Theatre when he was a playwriting student at the Yale School of Drama. *Pill Hill* has since been produced in theaters around the country, including the Hartford Stage, Philadelphia Theatre Company, Chicago Theatre Company, ETA Creative Arts Foundation, Chicago, Ensemble Theatre in Houston, Penumbra Theatre Company-St. Paul, Minnesota, Florida A & M University-Tallahassee, North Carolina A & T University-Raleigh, Coppin State University, Baltimore, Maryland, and the University of Arkansas at Pine Bluff, to name a few. In addition to its St. Paul production, Penumbra Theatre Company presented *Pill Hill* at the National Black Theatre Festival in Winston-Salem, North Carolina. Among the theaters that have won awards for their productions of *Pill Hill* are the Chicago Theatre Company *(Joseph Jefferson Award for Best Ensemble Performance)*, ETA Creative Arts Foundation *(Black Theatre Alliance Awards for Best Costume Design, Best Ensemble, Best Performance in an ensemble, Best Actor, and Best Direction)*, Karamu Theatre, Cleveland, Ohio *(Kieffer Award for best production)*, and New Horizons Theatre, Pittsburgh (Onyx Awards for best ensemble performance, lead actor, and lighting).

Staged readings and productions of Kelley's works have been presented at such places as Jubilee Theatre in Fort Worth in Texas *(Thruway Diaries)*, Plowshares Theatre, in Detroit, Michigan *(White Chocolate)*, Billie Holiday Theatre in New York City *(White Chocolate)*, Juneteenth Legacy Theatre in Louisville, Kentucky *(Faith Hope and Charity: The Story of Mary McLeod Bethune, Habeas Corpus, Driving While Black,* and *Ain't Got Time To*

Die), African American Theatre Program at the University of Louisville (*Thruway Diaries* and *Blue Vein Society*), Claflin University (*Driving While Black*), Paul Robeson Performing Arts Company in Syracuse, New York (*The Blue Vein Society, Thruway Diaries,* and others), and Wales, United Kingdom, University of Glamorgan at Pontypridd at the Theatres of Science Conference (*A Hero For McBride*), Center for the Arts in Homer, New York (*Beautiful Game),* and (*Faith, Hope and Charity: The Story of Mary McLeod Bethune,)* Christ Community Church in Cortland, New York.

Penumbra Theatre Company awarded Kelley the Cornerstone Competition playwriting award and the Yale School of Drama the Molly Kuhn Award for *Pill Hill.* Kelley is the recipient of the James Thurber Playwright-In-Residence award from the Thurber House in Columbus, Ohio, which was awarded during the spring of 1998. During that time, Kelley also served as playwright-in-residence at Ohio State University. Additional residencies include the Blue Mountain Center in Blue Mountain Lakes, New York; the Virginia Center for the Creative Arts in Mt. San Angelo, Virginia; Byrdcliffe Arts Colony in Woodstock, New York; Mary Anderson Center for the Arts in Mt. St. Francis, Indiana; and Yaddo in Saratoga Springs, New York.

Pill Hill was published by Dramatic Publications in 1995, and it was also anthologized in *New American Plays*, Heinemann Books, 1992. Two *Pill Hill* scenes appeared in *Best Monologues for Male Actors*, 1992. Kelley's article, "Playwright Gives Crux of Pill Hill," appeared in the *Philadelphia Inquirer* on January, 29, 1992, while another article, "Sidney Poitier: Heros Integrationniste," appeared in *Cinemaction,* Paris, France, 1988.

In addition to his work as a playwright, Kelley has performed at the school and community levels for most of his life. His first—and second-grade teachers put him on the stage, and he has been there—more or less—ever since. However, it was during the eighth grade that Kelley first performed James Weldon Johnson's "The Creation" from Johnson's book of sermon poems *God's Trombones* at the St. Luke Missionary Baptist Church in Turkey Scratch, Arkansas. Today, Kelley is known in the Cortland area for his performances of the works of Johnson and Martin Luther King, Jr. He has performed *I Have A Dream, I've Been to the Mountain Top,* and *Letter from the Birmingham Jail* for more than thirty years.

Kelley teaches Communication Studies and Africana Studies at the State University of New York (SUNY) College at Cortland where his favorite courses include Films of Spike Lee, African Americans in TV and Film, Human Communication, and Interviewing Principles and Practices. He has also taught a number of special topics courses, such as African American Women in Theatre, African American Theatre and Video Workshop, Screen writing and Films of Spike Lee for Teachers.

The Board of Trustees of the State University of New York promoted Kelley to the rank of Distinguished Service Professor in 2008 for his many years of outstanding service. He is also the recipient of the SUNY Chancellor's Award for Excellence in Research and Creative Activities. Kelley has served as the Honors Convocation Keynote Speaker and was the SUNY Cortland President's Scholars Inaugural Reception Keynote Speaker. Among other noted awards are the SUNY Cortland Dedicated Service Award, Africana Studies Department, the Twenty-fiftth Anniversary Award for distinguished service and dedication to the SUNY Cortland Gospel Choir, Office of Multicultural Life Unity Celebration Award, Cortland Educational Opportunity Program (EOP) Special Appreciation Award presented by the staff and students of the EOP Program, and the Tompkins Community College Appreciation Award from the Black Student Union.

Kelley received his PhD in Speech, with a concentration in Radio-TV-Film, from the University Michigan and his MFA in playwriting from the Yale School of Drama. He earned his MA in Speech from Arkansas at Fayetteville and his BA in Speech and Drama from Arkansas at Pine Bluff. He has also studied screen writing, playwriting and film script development at New York University. A graduate of M. M. Tate High School in Marvell, Kelley claims Turkey Scratch, Arkansas as home.

Current professional memberships include Dramatists Guild of America, Black Theatre Network, United University Professions, and Phi Kappa Phi National Honor Society.